Handy Cruise Companion

Julie Burgess

First published by Busybird Publishing 2018
Copyright © 2018 Julie Ann Burgess

ISBN
Print: 978-1-925830-91-0
Ebook: 978-1-925830-20-0

Julie Ann Burgess has asserted her right under the Copyright, Designs and Patents Act 1988 to be identified as the author of this work. The information in this book is based on the author's experiences and opinions. The publisher specifically disclaims responsibility for any adverse consequences, which may result from use of the information contained herein. Permission to use information has been sought by the author. Any breaches will be rectified in further editions of the book.

All rights reserved. No part of this publication may be reproduced, stored in or introduced into a retrieval system, or transmitted in any form, or by any means (electronic, mechanical, photocopying, recording or otherwise) without the prior written permission of the author. Any person who does any unauthorised act in relation to this publication may be liable to criminal prosecution and civil claims for damages. Enquiries should be made through the publisher.

Cover image: Kev Howlett, Busybird Publishing
Cover design: Busybird Publishing
Layout and typesetting: Busybird Publishing
Editor: Jessica Waters

Busybird Publishing
2/118 Para Road
Montmorency, Victoria
Australia 3094
www.busybird.com.au

Testimonials

Disclaimer: *Discretion is valued by our clients, testimonial are displayed respecting their privacy.*

'The advice Julie gave was so spot on! Her guidance made our trip so much better - we knew all of the best spots to visit without wasting time! Her advice was just what we needed for a well-rounded trip.'
  - Jane

'Julie always has a big smile and is super knowledgeable with a wealth of information to impart. We felt safe knowing that Julie was supporting our trip.'
  - Ms Roberts

'You gave us so much more confidence to go on our second cruise.'
  - Pat

'She's so funny and engaging - always ready with a joke but you just knew that she was looking out for us throughout the trip, ready to intervene if things got overwhelming. We just had the best time and in no small part to Julie's professional, happy and friendly outlook. Would definitely travel with Julie again.'
  - Mrs McC

'The advice was to take suction hooks for drying small items of clothing, swimwear etc. and to pack ginger lollies to help with queasiness.'
    – **Amy**

'The advice Jules gave was much appreciated and very helpful. She gave a thorough overview of what to expect during the entire cruise experience.'
    – **Mrs S**

'C and I learnt so much from you.'
    – **PS**

'Julie definitely has a passion for 'cruising' and is more than willing to share her personal experiences as well as many helpful ideas to make others' experiences as exciting and memorable as hers. She truly wants other people to enjoy cruising as much as she does.'
    – **Ms AS**

To my family and all the wonderful passengers and crew I have met over the years, you are my cruise family.

Contents

Introduction	i
1. Ship Ahoy	1
2. Healthy Sea Air	15
3. Where in the World?	27
4. Travel Trunk	43
5. All Aboard	57
6. Cruise Card	71
7. Salty Sea Dog	83
8. A Burly Chum	91
9. Iceberg!	103
10. Little Ship Mates	117
11. Ahoy, Me Hearty	129
12. Post Cruise Blues (PCB)	145
Biography	157
Resources	159
Jules Cruise Companion – Bucket List	161
Jules Cruise Companion – Children Cruise Packing List	163

Introduction

'I am a citizen of the most beautiful nation on earth, a nation whose laws are harsh yet simple, a nation that never cheats, which is immense and without borders, where life is lived in the present. In this limitless nation, this nation of wind, light, and peace, there is no other ruler besides the sea.'

~ Bernard Moitessier

The magic about this book is that it is aimed at *never-gonna* cruisers, *thinking-about-your-first-time* cruisers to *serial* cruisers. It is aimed to assist people with accessibility or medical challenges to see that cruising is an all-around wonderful holiday experience, which just needs a little more pre-planning. Anyone who had a cruise question or concern will find an answer in this book. What this book will do is show you where to spend money on experiences so you will have tales of adventure that you can share forever.

I will show you that you should never get so busy that you don't have time for a life. My first cruise experience was at the age of 21, on *Fairstar the Funship*. I slept 9 hours in 9 days on a Pacific Island cruise out of Sydney. I only have a few photos of that experience and they were all of me participating in something and my feet in the white sand of Mystery Island. I will show you how this one experience shaped my holiday choices. I will show you how you, too, can have thousands of memories and photos to share, as the fun never ends.

People ask me questions all the time about my cruise experiences, handy hints and hacks, so I decided to put them all in one place. Here at your fingertips, I have done all the hard yards. Just follow the guidance, relax and enjoy your cruise holiday. I will answer all the questions I have been asked and ones people haven't even thought of asking yet.

One question I am always asked is this: *Why would I go on a cruise and not just go on a land holiday?* There are two primary reasons: first, you unpack once; and the second is with a cruise you can wake up in a different place every morning and you did none of the hard work to get there.

Use these pages to guide you through your decision to book a cruise. We will go through step by step all the things to consider when looking for a cruise holiday. We will look at the planning, the packing, how to get to the cruise, what to do on the cruise and even what to expect when you return home.

This is your step-by-step journey to unforgettable memories with my help all the way. I will share with you my 30-plus cruise experience to help you get the most out of your cruise holiday. I will give you my top tips and hacks to make the whole holiday cruise smoothly. I share my personal experiences to the most common questions a novice cruiser would ask.

Cruising is accessible to everyone.

1
Ship Ahoy

'Once a year, go somewhere you've never been.'
~ Dalai Lama

Every year, more people are becoming interested in cruise holidays. Some people like a hassle-free holiday where everything's taken care of. Some people want to see a lot of different locations, while having a relaxing style of holiday. And some people might want to socialise, where some may want quiet time. All of these scenarios describe cruising. Cruising is for everyone and anyone.

When you compare cruise holidays with land-based holidays, you may find they are more affordable when you calculate the cost of accommodation, all meals and entertainment. More people are seeing that a cruise holiday is a great option. Yet still a lot of people have never had a cruise experience, for a lot of different reasons. This book will answer your questions, diminish any fears you may have, and guide you to see how easy and fun cruising can be.

The growth of the cruise industry shows no signs of slowing and you will see a steady introduction of new cruise ships and new itineraries to explore the world every year. As a novice cruiser it will add value if you have an overview of the cruise industry, its historical evolution, the present and the potential future of the industry. I will cover some of the things I would like to have known when I was starting out.

I have cruised with seven different cruise lines on 30+ cruises. In no particular order, I have enjoyed sailing with Princess, Carnival, P&O Australia, Celebrity, Norwegian, Disney Cruise Line and Royal Caribbean International. I am always asked, which one is the best cruise line? I have to say, there is no straight answer, it depends on what you want and what you can afford. My absolute favourite is Disney Cruise Line and I have been on all four of their current ships – Wonder, Magic, Dream and Fantasy. Why is Disney Cruise Line my favourite? The crew, the ships, the food, the shows, the characters, the exciting magical atmosphere. To me, there is nothing not to like.

There is a certain 'IT' factor, about cruising. It is unquantifiable, it just makes cruising unique. If you are not open to finding the 'IT' then don't waste your money, do not book a cruise. There is a magic that you will never understand.

When we think of cruising we may think of the majestic Cunard Queen Elizabeth or Queen Mary 2, or the current largest cruise ships, Royal Caribbean's Harmony or Allure of the Seas. Your memory may also prompt you to think of historical cruise ships that are synonymous with notable seafaring mishaps. The S.S. Titanic (1912) that hit an iceberg with the loss of an estimated 1522 souls and Costa Concordia (2012) that struck rocks, with the loss of 32 souls.

With modern cruising you don't need to know its history to enjoy fun on the ocean waves, however out of respect, it would be nice to have some understanding about the evolution of the fastest growing holiday sector. I count 6 embarkation ports in Australia and 31 in the USA and with 50 other countries with cruise ports, there would be up to 2000 ports for you to visit.

A good place to start talking about cruising would be to differentiate between the terms 'cruise ship' and 'ocean liner' with a reminder they should not be interchangeable, although the distinction between the term has blurred in recent times. An ocean liner is a ship designed to transport passengers from one point to another. A strongly built, steel hull vessel with long tapered bows, a deep draft designed to make the voyage calmer. Where a cruise ship is a large passenger ship, built for pleasure, it usually takes passenger to various ports or extended ocean cruising.

Ocean Travel of the 1800s
I am sure you have never given any thought to how the current cruise industry developed. From its origins in 1818 carrying cargo, the Black Ball Line founded a regular service from North America to Europe. This line eventually ferried thousands of immigrants from Europe to America. The Peninsular and Oriental Steam Navigation Company, founded in 1822 was the first company to advertise, seeking tourists to cruise in 1835.

1. Ship Ahoy

This company would eventually become P&O. A new age in comfort arrived to ocean travel with Cunard Line's *Britannia*, when it embarked on a 14-day transatlantic voyage from Liverpool with a live cow on board to supply passengers with fresh milk on July 4, 1840.

The first genuine leisure cruise occurred in 1844 when P&O Cruises sailed passengers from Southampton to the Mediterranean for the sole purpose of pleasure. P&O Cruises later expanded its itineraries to include the British Empire, the Orient, India, Australia and New Zealand. Urban legends have it that the most favoured cabins on a cruise ship came from the acronym of *port out, starboard home*, giving us the word POSH. As passengers going to the Far East, the port side was shaded from the sun, while returning home it was the starboard side.

From the 1850s, ships began to focus more on passenger comforts, including luxuries such as electric lights, more spacious deck areas and on-board entertainment. This era also saw the introduction of a steerage class where passengers were responsible for finding their own sleeping space and bringing their own food on board. The White Star Line founded in 1869 launched the *Oceanic* and *Adriatic*. Over the next few years the record for crossing the Atlantic fell from 14 to 8 to 5 days. In 1867, Mark Twain recorded his six-month experience in his novel *Innocents Abroad* when he was a passenger on the first cruise to begin in America. And in 1897 the British Medical Journal wrote that a cruise to the West Indies provides 'opportunities for recovering health', as 'the most delightful days of peace and leisure may be passed doing nothing...' Both of these endorsements acted to cement the idea of cruising into popular culture. With rapid expansion in the late 19th century, as larger luxurious ships were commissioned.

The 1900s

Welcome to the era of the joy of ocean travel. Passengers travelled in hotel style ships, between Europe and America, before the advent of long distance aircraft travel. In 1904, P&O launched the *Vectis* as its first cruise ship, with shore excursions facilitated by Thomas Cook. The romance of cruising continued to develop with companies such as Cunard forging the tradition of dressing for dinner and on-board entertainment. The three Olympic-class ocean liners of the White Star Line aimed to be the most luxurious. As history shows they did not reach their potential with the sinking of *S.S. Titanic* in 1912, *Britannic* being sunk by a mine during World War I and *Olympic* scrapped in 1936. During World War I in 1915 to 1918 a variety of cruise lines were sunk including Cunard *Lusitania* and Italian Liner *Ancona*.

The first world cruise was made by *Laconia*, a British Cunard Line and lasted six months in 1922. The Great Depression saw the two rivals Cunard Line and White Star Line merging in 1934. Between 1939 and 1945, during World War II, many cruise ships were requestioned and used to transport troops including the *Queen Mary*, *Aquitania* and the *Queen Elizabeth*, many being bombed and destroyed.

In October, 1958, the first Transatlantic commercial Boeing 747s reduced transatlantic travel time from six days by passenger liner to around six hours. This meant there was a move away from ocean liners as a form of transportation, resulting in ocean travel being promoted as a holiday in its own right during the 1960s.

By the 1970s, it was no longer fashionable, practical, or economical to travel by boat. In 1974, the Cunard Line was the only company running transatlantic services between New York and London. The QE2 remains one of the fastest passenger liners afloat according to Wikipedia, with a maximum cruising speed of 38 knots. While it was fast enough to cross the Atlantic in just four days, it was elegant enough to stage big productions. Regardless of the berths passengers booked, they enjoyed the same service, menus, international celebrity entertainment, and activities. The concept of this style of cruising caught on, and the general public began taking cruises for short vacations, rather than solely as a means of transportation.

Of course, it would only be fair to also give credit to the creators of the original infomercial, 'Love Boat' in the 1970s. The television series generated a resurgence in cruising's popularity.

While the show's story lines were made of Hollywood tripe, its gorgeous scenery and exotic ports of call had an undeniable impact on millions of viewers every week. Filmed on *Pacific Princess* from Princess Cruise Line, the focus was on itineraries to tropical destinations at a time that cruise ship amenities began to evolve. Pools, casinos and on-board entertainment all became standard as more cruise ships were being built to new specifications for the emerging leisure markets. Michael Grace, a writer of the Love Boat during the mid-80s, desensitised the general public idea that cruising was only accessible to the rich and famous. This inspired ordinary people to cruise, creating the cruise industry as we know it today. With unrealistic storylines of romance and fantasy, it was an international marketing campaign cementing the empire that is Carnival Corp, formalising Love Boat's iconic status.

Cruising is a major part of the tourism sector in the US and Australia and it has reached a level of enormous significance world-wide. The increase in destinations and ports of call around the world, a multinational on-board personnel and passengers from every continent, has important economic, environmental, legal, and social implications. Until 1975-1980, cruises offered shuffleboard, deck chairs, and fancy cocktails. After 1980, they offered increasing amenities.

Cruising is no longer limited to the calm waters of the Caribbean and the Mediterranean. Consequently, cruise ships have to be able to handle much more difficult oceanic conditions, and are now taking on the characteristics of ocean liners, becoming stronger, faster and more hydrodynamic. Royal Caribbean's Radiance-class ships and NCL's Jewel-class cruise ships can achieve speeds that rival some classic ocean liners. Other cruise lines soon launched similar ships, such as Carnival Cruise Line's Fantasy-class, leading up to the Panamax-type Vista-class operated by P&O, Holland America and Cunard.

The first dedicated cruise ships that emerged during the 1970s could carry about 1000 passengers, and by the 1980s, expanded to more than 2,000 passengers. For example, Royal Caribbean developed different classes of ships including Sovereign-, Vision-, Radiance-, and Freedom-class for between 2,500 to

3,500 passengers. Its revolutionary Oasis-class are currently the world's largest passenger ships, carrying up to 6,296 guests and approximately 2,200 crew members. So, in two short decades the largest class cruise ships have grown longer by about 100 metres, almost doubled in width, and doubled the total passengers they could carry. The ten largest cruise ships in 2017 include Royal Caribbean's Liberty-, Ovation-, Anthem- Quantum-, Oasis-, Allure-, Harmony of the Seas, and Norwegian Cruise Line's Joy, Escape and Epic.

As mentioned before, cruise ships are often requisitioned during times of war, for example during the Falklands War as hospital ships or troop transport. During major events such as the 2004 Olympics in Athens, cruise ships were used as additional accommodation, and during Hurricane Katrina in 2005, Carnival Fantasy, Carnival Holiday and Carnival Sensation were used to house evacuees.

Cruise Industry Consolidation
Historically, there have been several diverse events that have shaped the cruise industry consolidation, such the Iraq and Kosovo wars, the Achille Lauro hijack in 1985, and September 11. A string of bankruptcy in the 2000s left the market wide open for the largest cruise companies such as Royal Caribbean Cruise Limited, Carnival Corporation, and Star Cruises to consolidate into enormous corporations. The undisputed leader is Carnival Corporation, with headquarters in Miami and London, with 12 cruise brands in Australia, Europe and North America, operating over 90 cruise ships, with around 65,000 shipboard employees and servicing over 170,000 guests at any given time.

Cruising as a global industry offers both domestic and international holidaying choices. The number of companies and the amount of ships give a variety of itineraries to choose from. The cruise industry almost tripled in the last 15 years and is expected to continue to grow steadily despite economic growth cycles and recessions. The Global Financial Crisis of 2008-2009 had no real impact on cruise demand.

Operators, Cruise Lines and Cruise Industry Competition

The cruise industry makes up about half of all ocean and coast transportation. The four largest cruise shipping companies, Carnival Lines, Royal Caribbean, Norwegian Cruise Line and MSC Cruises account for over 95% of the market. Of that market, Carnival control close to half of the market and Royal Caribbean around a quarter. As most cruise companies have been acquired by parent companies, they keep their individual names to protect differentiation. For example, Royal Caribbean Cruises is serviced under 6 different brands including Celebrity Cruises, Carnival, Princess, and Azura Club Cruises, all catering for different markets.

Cruise line brands partly exist because of repeat customer loyalty, and also to offer different levels of service and quality. Cruise industry competition allows diverse strategies and plans to identify and specialise in the specific markets, resulting in a well-defined division of the cruise industry market niches such as luxury, premium and contemporary. Each one offers diversified and targeted cruise products and services to satisfy both mass consumer market budget packages.

Foreign Flagged Cruise Ships or Flags of Convenience

While cruise line headquarters are predominantly based in the United States, at the moment nearly all major cruise lines use ships built in Italy, France or Germany, that are then registered in countries with less onerous requirements on employers, such as Panama, Malta or Bermuda. This is to get around US labour and taxation laws. Nearly all large cruise ships are staffed with international crews and cruise under a foreign flag – also called a Flag of Convenience.

At any one time there could be between fifty to eighty different nationalities of crew working on a cruise ship. This crew is governed by the 'Seafarers Bill of Rights' or the International Labour organisation's 2006 Maritime Labour Convention which provides comprehensive rights and protections for crewmembers. The standards relate to working hours, rest pauses, health and safety etc. This form of employment has been around since the early 1900s, borne out of the Passenger Service

Act of 1886. This U.S. law forbids foreign-flagged vessels from transporting passengers on one-way journeys between ports in the United States, and while it was intended to assist the shipbuilding industry, in reality it did the opposite.

To register a ship in the United States, it is required to be built in the country and staffed with an American crew, therefore having to comply with U.S. employment regulations and pay correct American wages. This is extremely expensive compared to using employees from developing countries who will work for less money. You will find that cruises around Hawaii will typically be more expensive because cruise companies are required to register their ships in the United States and employ unionised crew. You may notice that when a foreign-flagged cruise ship leaves an American port it often takes a strange route. This is to circumvent the restriction created by the Passenger Service Act. For example, sailing from San Diego or Los Angeles, the ship must first visit Ensenada, Mexico, before travelling to Hawaii. Almost all cruises to Alaska visit a Canadian port. This law may change in the future which would open up different itinerary possibilities.

Naming Convention of Ships
It is not uncommon for a ship to morph through different identities under different ownership. Through a transfer of ownership process, ships are renamed and refitted. For example, in Australia, P&O ARIA and EDEN were once Holland America Ryndam and Statendam respectively.

Consistent naming conventions allow easy recognition of the cruise line, for example the use of a prefix or suffix within the name. Some cruise lines will use their brand name as a prefix, to represent the respective cruise line. For example, Norwegian STAR, Disney Fantasy and Carnival Sensation. P&O Cruises Australia uses the prefix 'Pacific', i.e. Pacific Aria or Pacific Dawn.

A suffix such as 'Princess' denotes the Princess Cruise Line, i.e. Coral Princess. Other companies may use a consistent suffix. Royal Caribbean International uses *of the Seas*, i.e. Voyage of the Seas. Holland America has used the suffix 'dam' on all their ships since 1883, i.e. Westerdam.

This can allow for similar names of ships over different cruise lines, so be careful to not get confused.

Environmental Impact

With several thousand passengers and crew visiting ports, environmental considerations are now playing a more important role. Cruise ships generate large volumes of a number of waste streams that can result in discharges to the marine environment, including sewage, graywater, ballast water, hazardous wastes, solid waste, oily bilge water, and air pollutants. A cruise ship adds additional stress onto the utilities of municipalities. Different ships generate variation CO_2 emissions, based on their age, size and the ship's capacity configuration. Shore side power (Cold Ironing) facilities have been installed in a number of urban cruise terminals in an expectation of reducing ships' environmental impact. To cut emissions, the port of Juneau in Alaska was the first in the world to offer shore side power in 2001. This allows the cruise vessel to connect ships to the power grid so they can turn off their engines while docked. This saves an estimated 17,000 litres of fuel in a 10 hour docking period. Other US and European ports have now followed suit.

Future

The trends underlining the cruise industry have so far been supply based, meaning the ships are being built and the customers are found to fill them through various marketing and discounting strategies. Demand in the cruise industry is created through pricing, branding and marketing. Cruise operators have to develop a competitive cruise product which includes quality on-board facilities, combined with cultural shore excursions and tourist sites within easy access from the ship.

The construction of cruise ships tends to be a cycle, where several ships are ordered and enter into service within a short timeframe. So far cruise companies have been successful in finding customers to fill the increased capacity of the larger ships. Cruise products become diversified to attract new customers and to respond to the preferences of a wide array of customer groups. Most cruise lines work around specific cruise themes and voyage lengths can vary to meet the changing holiday patterns of customers.

The main market for cruising is the older demographic, and this will continue with the aging population. This is an irony, as cruise customers are getting significantly younger. In 1995 the average age of a cruiser was about 65 years. Then it moved to 56 in 2002, 50 in 2011, 49 in 2014 and the ripe 'old' age of 46 in 2015, according to Cruise Lines International Association (CLIA). Globally it has remained at 46 during 2017, the lowest in 20 years. This has not stopped some cruise lines trying different methods to entice younger travellers looking for romance on the high seas.

What is novel with the cruise industry is that the ship itself represents the destination, essentially acting as a floating hotel (or a theme park) with all the related facilities (bars, restaurants, theatres, casinos, swimming pools, etc.). Some cruise lines continue to innovate new entertainment concepts on board their vessels, including surf pools, water parks, planetariums, golf simulators, on-deck LED movie screens, multi-room villas with private pools and in-suite Jacuzzis, ice-skating rinks, rock-climbing walls, bungee trampolines and more.

For the past few decades, cruise line companies have invested millions of dollars into ordering new and innovative ships that will increase the available cruise capacity. Some newer ships have the capacity for close to 6,000 passengers and around 2,100 crew. In 2016 there were 315 ships worldwide, with a passenger capacity of 23.6 million combined. Cruise Industry News predicts the current 2018 global capacity of 27 million passengers will get close to 40 million passengers by 2027, with a fleet of 472 ships.

The future of the cruise industry looks strong as global economies improve, with China, Europe and Australia expected to be growing markets. I can see exciting developments for new itineraries in emerging markets in Asia, the Middle East, Amazon and Brazil, Greenland and the Antarctic regions, and an increase in US, Canadian and Australian domestic ports.

The cruise industry offers continual developments in an effort to lure first-time cruisers on board. If you want more than shipboard pampering, and want to experience foreign cultures or learning new hobbies, you will find these on board. You can also find programs offering everything from art to music, culture, geography, photography or even oceanography.

If sailing on huge ships is not your thing, consider a smaller cruise line. Small luxury vessels service exotic locations such as Asia and South America. There are yachts and sailboats that carry only 10 to 30 passengers, to smaller ships and romantic, five-masted sailing vessels that carry around 200 passengers.

The cost of fuel will influence transatlantic crossings in the future, so a slower cruise will save money lengthening a crossing by one day. As the cruise industry is driven by supply, it is likely that supply saturation will occur where the number of cruise lines and ships has reached capacity that further growth has to come from improvements and developments.

As the cruise industry expands to provide more options for passengers, niche market itineraries such as the Arctic or Antarctica will command higher prices than in the mass market competition of areas such as the South Pacific, Caribbean or Mediterranean. You can see a move now to offering a floating hotel concept, as some cruise lines offer longer shore stay options where the cruise ship aims to berth near major sporting events (such as Melbourne Cup, the State of Origin, the British Open, the Rio Carnival or the Monaco Grand Prix).

In the future more consideration will need to be paid to the environmental, social and economic impact of large volumes of tourists visiting small communities. There may be a move away from hub ports to smaller 'must see' ports for cruisers wanting a diverse experience with a regional and more authentic cultural experience.

To combat some of the negative consequences of a mass influx of tourists to ports and communities, the cruise industry may become more involved in terminal operations, such as investing in private ports or resorts. In the future we may see new cruise terminals co-located with service amenities such shopping precincts, hotels, tourist attractions such as theme parks. From the 1990s, cruise lines have introduced 'Private Islands', mostly operating in the Caribbean, delivering different economic benefits by providing an alternative to traditional congested ports. This is a monopolistic control over local stores and services, open and available round-the-clock while the cruise ship is docked. This eliminates any competition and provides a control that ensures a positive experience for passengers.

All Hands on Deck:
- Go to your local travel agent and pick up some colour cruise brochures
- Watch Mighty Ships episodes on the Discovery Channel: www.discovery.ca/Shows/Mighty-Cruise-Ships
- Mighty Cruise Ships documentaries on the Smithsonian Channel: www.smithsonianchannel.com/shows/mighty-cruise-ships/1003687
- Google different cruise companies and look at the variety of itineraries.

2

Healthy Sea Air

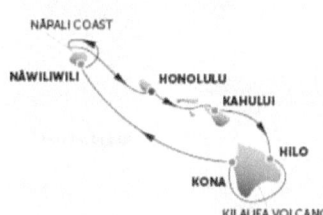

Date	Port	Arrive	Depart
Saturday, August 24	Honolulu, Oahu, HI		7:00pm
Sunday, August 25	Kahului, Maui, HI	8:00am	
Monday, August 26	Kahului, Maui, HI		6:00pm
Tuesday, August 27	Hilo, Hawaii, HI	8:00am	6:00pm
Wednesday, August 28	Kona, Hawaii, HI	7:00am	5:30pm
Thursday, August 29	Nawiliwili, Kauai, HI	10:00am	
Friday, August 30	Nawiliwili, Kauai, HI / At Sea		2:00pm
Saturday, August 31	Honolulu, Oahu, HI	7:00am	

'The planning stage of a cruise is often just as enjoyable as the voyage itself, letting one's imagination loose on all kinds of possibilities. Yet translating dreams into reality means a lot of practical questions have to be answered.'

~ Jimmy Cornell

As amazing as travelling is, don't leave it to your later years to really explore the world, do it now while you can. Cruising is not only fun, full of new experiences, adventures, and memories that last a lifetime, there are also a variety of personal benefits. Research shows travel offers health benefits for your mind, body, and soul. It may lower stress, help work productivity, lead to better relationships, boost brain health, and reduce the risk of depression and heart attacks.

Mark Twain, who sailed around the coast of the Mediterranean in 1869, wrote a travelogue, *Innocents Abroad*. This leaves you with the powerful message that 'Twenty years from now you will be more disappointed by the things that you didn't do than by the ones you did do. So throw off the bowlines. Sail away from the safe harbor. Catch the trade winds in your sails. Explore. Dream. Discover.' Are you open to Twain's message or does it fall on deaf ears? As the saying goes, 'The world is a book; those who do not travel read only a page', which one do you choose? Will you read the whole book or just stay on that one page?

The strongest piece of advice I give people is to experience more joy in life through cruising and travel. It is not just about short weekend trips or organised tours. Take an extended, meaningful journey to somewhere you've never gone before, out of your comfort zone and with an open schedule. Open your heart and mind to what the universe has in store for you. Take time to wait and listen for the opportunities that await you. A sense of wanderlust, a longing for more destinations, food, cultures to experience, and people to meet.

When you read articles about the advantages of travel, you see commentators come up with lists of Top 5 or Top 15 benefits to travel. There are some core themes, but in reality the benefits of cruising are immeasurable. I want to inspire you to cruise and holiday more, so I have created my own list of the 31 benefits of cruising and travel

Let me demonstrate the wonderful benefits that I see that cruising has done for me.

1. **Cruising improves heart health.** I feel that cruising has kept me pretty healthy and I am hoping it increases my life expectancy. I hope it decreases my risk of heart attack, depression and cognitive loss. I want to live for a long time having fun.

2. **Cruising keeps me fit.** I know that cruising has made me fitter. I lost 5kg in 3 months without trying. I was just walking more and using stairs while exploring the world. Walking on different terrain such as uneven surfaces or a beach, makes your muscles work twice as hard.

3. **Cruising can reduce the risk of cognitive deterioration.** I am hoping that by using my brain continually, to plan and go on cruising, will slow down or reduce my risk of developing dementia. By engaging with people and being stimulated I hope I can stave off cognitive deterioration. When facing new and challenging situations I have learnt to be flexible and adapt. Cruising has made me become more culturally aware, by connecting and engaging with new people, cultures, situations, and experiences.

4. **Cruising improves relaxation.** For me, cruising recharges my energy levels and I feel happier and relaxed when I get home. I am invigorated, rejuvenated and experience improved moods. Cruising helps me deal with the general stresses of everyday life.

5. **Cruising boosts mental health.** Though stress is normal, too much can be detrimental to your health. It is unrealistic to think you can have a stress-free life. I know I feel less stressed almost instantly when I start to cruise. The change of environment, signals something in my body and brain. Since I started cruising over 15 years ago, I would say I have less periods of low mood or depression. Other than moments of extreme events in my life, I feel more optimistic and generally more satisfied in my day to day life.

6. **Cruising enhances creativity**. Since I have been cruising I have made over 15 coffee table photobooks, started a YouTube channel and written a book. I want to share my experiences to inspire others to have a great time.

7. **Cruising enhances friendships.** I have been privileged to meet people from around the world while travelling, stay in touch and even visit them later. By staying with people and engaging with other cultures it has humbled and inspired me. I always try to stay away from tourist areas and aim to stay where I can have an authentic local experience. I immerse myself in culture and adapt and adopt some local traditions. By spending time with locals you get to hear their philosophies and perspectives which broadens my frames of reference.

8. **Cruising increases knowledge and cultural awareness.** The more I cruise the more knowledgeable and culturally aware I become. I have had opportunities to form lifelong memories by sharing experiences, exploring new cultures and food with strangers who have become good friends.

9. **Cruising keeps you learning.** I have learnt more about the world through cruising than I ever could have from formal education. I have spoken to people who have lived through some of modern history's critical events, such as wars and natural disasters. I have learnt more from those conversations than any textbook or news broadcast.

10. **Cruising creates a lifetime of memories.** Through cruising I have connected with so many people all over the world. Many of those connections have continued to flourish for years after the cruise ended. Creating the photo books allows me to relive the experience as well as share it with others. New friends with unique personalities brings new perspectives into my life. I have built meaningful relationships with my philosophy of Open Heart, Open Mind. I am choosing to live while I can, and cruise as much of this amazing planet as I can.

11. **Cruising can build self-confidence.** Cruising has allowed me to accomplish so much, I have learnt to adapt to changing situations and in doing so built my confidence. I have pushed myself physically and psychologically out of my comfort zone to explore new countries and cultures. I have visited the Costa Rican jungle, ancient Petra and Olympia, Europe, Scandinavia, Russia and more. I set goals for myself and push myself to achieve them, for example getting fitter to revisit Jordan after a cruise visit.

12. **Cruising makes you more trusting and increases your faith in humanity**. I believe that all people of the world want peace and a good life with their family. The more people I meet from different nations, the more commonalities and similar needs I see between us. My perspectives have changed over the years as I have become close friends with people of different backgrounds and cultures. As I cruise the wider world I am more aware of where I fit into it, and not just a narrow perspective of my own culture. By cruising I break out of my cultural bubble and explore other nations. If you allow it, cruising opens your mind to other ways of thinking and feeling. Cruising and exploring other cultures can also make you appreciate your own world.

13. **Cruising the world has made me realise how little I know about the world and in reality that my home is the whole world.** When I cruise I realise that my home is really the whole world. I see the importance of living in harmony with other people and the planet. To be a true citizen of the world you can't stay in your own town, state or country. Cruising has taught me the world is not as dangerous as the mass media presents. Every new cultural cruise experience is another piece in the tapestry of my life. Every person I meet has the potential to become a friend.

14. **Cruising has made me a better problem solver.** From planning a cruise, to the execution, and eventually returning home, has all allowed me to get to know myself better. I developed versatile problem-solving

skills and my mind is more open to alternate solutions when I am confronted with a problem or new situation. I am less reactionary and more resourceful when faced with a problem, and I have built my creativity and problem-solving ideas by getting out of my comfort zone. Cruising and travel has given me the tools to overcome obstacles and better cope with life, opening me up to embrace change with little resistance.

15. **Cruising has improved my social and communication skills.** Continually being away from my normal environment, I have had to develop advanced communication skills to achieve the simplest of activities. From finding a bathroom or restaurant, to checking directions, I have learnt some valuable skills to communicate when there is a language difference, and I know I need to be clear in my message to be understood correctly. Language barriers give me an opportunity to explore new languages, while I work on other forms of communication such as hand signals.

16. **Cruising has made me healthier.** Cruising gets me out and about in nature and the fresh air, something I don't normally do when I am at home. Walking on deck or out on excursions gives me a boost of Vitamin D. It helps me with my mood, my mental health and I hope it is helping with my blood pressure and reducing risks of other health conditions such as heart disease.

17. **Travel can boost your immunity**. By going to my travel doctor every year I religiously maintain my standard immunisation schedule such as MMR (Measles, Mumps & Rubella), TDaP (Tetanus, Diphtheria & Pertussis) and Hep A. Cruising has exposed me to different environments, including different air quality, food and water supplies, which has created stronger antibodies and naturally boosted my immune system. Notwithstanding, you should never forgo normal hygiene practices to boost your immunity while cruising, so you should still wash

your hands or use a little hand sanitiser occasionally. Remember that nothing is more important than drinking clean water, so please don't test out your immunity by drinking anything that is suspect.

18. **Cruising has made me humble.** The world is full of amazing natural and man-made wonders and I often find myself in awe of such things. I was in a Norwegian Fjord once with a group of Americans, where one guy voiced less than positive sentiments of the vista. I asked, 'What would you prefer? A Disney reproduction or seeing the forces of a million years of nature?' Point taken. I feel I have a duty to respect the culture of the places and people you visit. Some have very traditional customs and beliefs, where others are more modern. Experiencing different cultures can be an enlightening, humbling and educational experience. As I cruise the world and visit developing nations I have learned to appreciate the luxuries we have such as running water and electricity.

19. **Cruising has expanded my horizons and given me new perspective**. Cruising has given me the opportunity to shape and change my personality, especially with my mantra of Open Heart, Open Mind. I have learnt that I need to be self-reliant and I need to be able to follow through and complete tasks without relying on anyone. I have become more open to new experiences, developed better skills to get along with people, and my social network has expanded exponentially. My values and perspectives have changed by continually putting myself into personally challenging situations. Through observations and talking to people, my views have broadened as I challenge my assumptions, and explore alternative ways of thinking.

20. **Cruising has helped me reinvent myself**. We all search for meaning and purpose, and cruising has allowed me to look at my life from a distance. By taking stock of what I see, I have more clarity and a sense of purpose, especially as I transition to being an empty nester and regain my independence.

21. **Cruising has increased my connections to others and myself.** By cruising I have met people from all over the world that I might never have had an opportunity to meet. From those chance encounters I have established amazing deep friendships. I would like to think that my mental and physical health has also improved by meeting all those wonderful people.

22. **Cruising can boost your relationships and can bring back the romance!** As a solo cruiser, I cannot reflect on the potential benefits to rekindling romance between couples, although I can see how it could happen, being relaxed, maybe communicating more and creating new memories. I know that cruising has brought some wonderful people into my life and that I am very happy with the relationships that have been formed.

23. **Cruising makes it really easy to make friends**. I have a saying, 'I collect people, not souvenirs.' There is a magic when you can be yourself and people accept you as you are. I find it easy to be my authentic self when cruising and start conversations with strangers who become fast friends. At times I think it is easier to make friends when travelling than at home as people are more open and willing to talk, have a relaxed mindset and are there to meet people too.

24. **Cruising makes you fearless** because when you are on holidays you do things that are out of your comfort zones. When you travel, you do not care what you do at all and you can just break free and have fun from the norm, regardless of age. Be warned, this fearlessness gets stronger the more you travel.

25. **Cruising makes you happier.** I always feel happy planning a cruise, as it is part of the whole experience. Exploring the world is fun, even a small break like a short cruise is a break from my normal routine which makes me feel good. In reality, any time you nourish your soul will inadvertently experience some positive feelings. To me, any cruise adventure will create new, happy memories that will last a lifetime.

26. **Cruising makes you better in the workplace.** I know I feel better about work when I am about to go on a cruise, or have just returned from one. The feel-good hormones released make me feel more productive, upbeat and energetic. Being relaxed after my cruise extends to the weeks following my return home.

27. **Cruising makes you more patient and tolerant.** When you cruise you have absolutely no power to influence some situations. Accepting things are out of you control won't kill you, and the earth will still turn, so embrace the experience as character building gifts from the universe. Dealing with missing flights, delays, booking on the wrong dates and cultural differences during my years of cruising has made me a more tolerant, patient and understanding person.

28. **Cruising can help you get over a loss.** When you experience great change in your life, taking charge of your choices and going on a cruise can help find yourself. When I am cruising I find it to be a character building experience. As I disconnect from my normal life I can take the time to focus and fully recharge myself.

29. **Taking a cruise can give you an opportunity to find a new purpose.** Cruising is an investment in yourself. I find it gives me purpose and direction in my life. As I travel and experience more of the world, I am filled with gratitude and appreciation from all the experiences. So I say, cruise now while you have your health. Life is a wonderful gift. Don't wait for the regret of saying, 'I wish I had'. I live for today and say, 'I'm glad I did'.

30. **Cruising is invigorating.** Cruising can reduce stress, tension and restore balance and happiness to your life. You can travel to a location that has extra healing potential, such as the natural hot springs of Turkey, the Dead Sea, Iceland or Costa Rica. Bathing in mineral-rich waters can improve your stress, your pain levels and your skin. There are some famous energy vortexes over the world including Stonehenge, Sedona, Arizona, and Mount Desert Island, Maine.

31. It's never been this cheap to cruise. With the internet and all the new technology, you can plan your ideal trip. From your budget, the duration of the trip and what you want to do, you can find a trip that exactly suits you. Read the blog and get inspired. There will never be a better time to book.

The take home message is stop making excuses! Travelling should be a priority – start planning your cruise as soon as possible!

All Hands on Deck:
- Find a cruise blogger that you like and follow them
- Read about other people's experiences
- Talk to family and friends about their cruise experiences.

3

Where in the World?

'Land was created to provide a place for boats to visit.'
~ Brooks Atkinson

If you have a Bucket List, cruising could be your vehicle to the seeing the world. Cruising offers choice, variety, and a one stop shop where you only unpack your suitcase once. In this chapter we will look at choosing a cruise itinerary, choosing a ship, choosing a stateroom, and more. You will discover how to find a cruise bargain, and I will guide you along your way as you plan your cruise.

First time cruisers, should be careful to not select their cruise experience based on price alone. The experience on a low end cruise may be too confronting or extreme for an inexperienced cruiser. It would not be a bargain if you did not enjoy the experience. So choosing the right cruise line for you is an important decision.

Different cruise lines appeal to different demographics. You might not enjoy being the youngest person on board ready to party when all other passengers are heading for bed. Spending some time investigating your cruise options will increase your chances of having a memorable and enjoyable experience. The more you read and talk to different cruise providers, you will find that not all ships are the same. Price points and facilities vary, and you have to maintain realistic expectations and decide where you sit on a wonderful cruise spectrum.

If you are looking for a cruise bargain you can look at different cruise lines as some are more affordable than others, so it pays to look at all of them before making a decision.

When looking for a cruise itinerary there are a few things you need to consider, such as when the cruise is available and if you want to return to the same port you departed from. Cruise lines sell destination itineraries that can be perennial, seasonal or repositionable.

Perennial. This is when a region is covered by an itinerary service throughout the year, with resilient demand. This is often attributed to stable, usually subtropical weather conditions, such as the Pacific Islands, the Caribbean or the Mediterranean.

Seasonal. Some regions have periods or seasons that are influenced by factors such as favourable weather conditions. For example, Norway, the Arctic Circle, the Baltic, and Alaska, can only be serviced during their hemisphere's summer months.

Repositioning. This is my secret. Shh! Repositioning (Repo) is my favourite type of cruising. As some itineraries are seasonal, the cruise companies have to move their ships between regions. These cruises are often offered at a lower rate as there is the additional cost of the travel arrangements and inconvenience following the cruise. These occur twice a year for the beginning or end of a ship's seasonal deployment. Repositioning itineraries can include Trans-Atlantic, Alaska to Hawaii, Panama Canal, Suez Canal or Trans Pacific.

There are pros and cons to going on a Repo cruise as the ships spend a long time at sea for less money. This is because there are less ports, so this means less port fees and taxes. Ships can also travel slower, and therefore use less fuel. You also have to get yourself to and from two different ports.

Repositioning cruises are reasonably priced with an added advantage (or disadvantage) of different weather conditions, a lot of sea days, and some reduced on board facilities. It is all a matter of perspective.

Cruise Port

A cruise from a close home port can be more economical. When finding a cheap cruise in another state or overseas, the value is often lost when the cost of the flights, ground transfers, pre- and post-cruise accommodation are factored in.

In addition to cruise lines selling destinations, they are now selling itineraries allowing for flexibility on choosing a port. There has been a growing number of ports where passengers may choose to begin or end their journey at a hub port. These hub ports (also called turn ports) such as Fort Lauderdale, Sydney and Singapore. These all are well served by both the cruise facilities, train and airport facilities, and can become a destination in themselves. Then there are gateway ports such as Civitavecchia, with no great tourist significance though it services the major tourist city of Rome.

Other cruise ports of call fall into different categories. This depends on the role they serve within their regions:

- **Destination port:** Where there are few, if any, excursions taking place outside the port area. Here, the port area is the sole destination, such as Venice, Barcelona, Kotor, Montenegro and Bergen Norway.
- **Balanced port:** Offering a combination of port area amenities as well as inland excursions, such as Miami or San Juan.

Home Port

Cruise lines plan ship itineraries years in advance. Ships are allocated to home ports for extended periods of time. For example, P&O Pacific Dawn's home port is Brisbane, and NCL Pride of America's home port is Honolulu. The planning for a cruise to turn-around takes months. The services required include the on loading of stores and provisions and the offloading of waste.

Length of a Cruise

A standard cruise itinerary is a loop beginning and ending at a hub port. These cruises typically last about 7 days and include around 3 to 5 ports of call depending on their respective proximity. There are shorter cruises from 1 to 4 nights that often just sail around in the ocean – 'A cruise to nowhere' – and not go to any ports, or may go to one port. Medium length cruises of 10 to 21 days are also offered in places such as New Zealand or Papua New Guinea. Longer cruises are more than 30 days, for example around Australia, and a full, Around the World itinerary is about 104 to 180 days. Around the World itineraries also allow you to purchase smaller segments.

Itinerary

It may be mercenary to say, if you want a deal, book a cruise after a crisis or natural disaster. People get nervous about travelling to trouble spots, and those fears are impacting cruise bookings. Rates can drop on certain sailings, especially close to the sail dates if ships aren't full. The newest ships doing summer or seasonal itineraries are generally the more sought after. With such competition and so many ships in a region there may be bargains for flexible cruisers.

When you are choosing an itinerary you may decide to look at Caribbean itineraries, as they may be a mixed bag for the next few years, as they recover from natural disasters of 2017. The Caribbean will always be popular given its proximity to the US market. You may find deals for cruises in October, November and December (before Christmas), as it is hurricane season.

Peak Season

When looking for a cruise bargain, avoid peak times, including the summer, school holidays, Christmas and Easter, as they are more expensive. Cruise prices are higher in peak season as there is more demand. I have not seen much discounting during these periods. If you are only available to travel during peak season, book the cruise date and cabin at the price you are willing to spend. If you only want a balcony or a suite, book it early or you may miss out.

Shoulder Season

For those who can cruise at any time of the year, you can find some great deals offered in the low or off-season, including winter itineraries in the Mediterranean. When you are looking for cruise bargains, look for cruises that take place in 'shoulder seasons', including February and late October. Often the first and last two weeks of a cruise season such as Alaska or the Baltic are more reasonably priced as the weather can be unpredictable.

Cruise Regions

With up to 2000 ports worldwide you will find at least one cruise that meets most of your needs. Cruise lines have itineraries to the Mediterranean, Caribbean, Alaska, Mexico, Northern Europe, Baltic and Northern Circle, South Pacific, Australia New Zealand, Asia, Middle East, South America and Antarctica.

Themed Cruises

When you are looking around the internet or talking to a travel agent for cruise options you will come across different themed cruises. Over the last 5 years or more, different promoters have hired headline performers, such as Jimmy Barnes, Dame Kiri Te Kanawa, John Williamson and Lee Kernighan on cruises called Rock the Boat, Country Cruisin', Bravo (Opera), and Groove Cruise (Pop Rock). You can cruise to Melbourne for the Melbourne Cup, or Sydney or Brisbane for the State of Origin.

Conference Cruises

Depending on your type of work, you may find that promoters also book rooms on cruise lines for use as conference space. Conference conveners will work through a designated travel agency to facilitate conference registration and stateroom selection.

Special Events

Over the years you get to share in other people's holiday fun. On most cruises you will find people celebrating birthdays, anniversaries and even weddings. It is not uncommon to see large groups of people sporting the same t-shirt, for example with the name of the event and the date and ship's name. I know of one group that planned to board the ship in secret to surprise a birthday boy.

Overall Slush Fund

Don't forget all the costs that add up to cover a cruise. The base cruise fee includes accommodation, food and entertainment on board. Other costs can add up when you're on board a cruise ship, like drinks, shore excursions, shopping, spa treatments and casino. Those who are planning to drink a lot of the hard stuff may want to consider a beverage package, if it's not already an all-inclusive journey. You also have to budget for tips for the crew (if they are accepted). To see how much to budget for tips and gratuities, read my blog post at:

> www.julescruisecompanion.com.au/tipping-and-gratuities

When you are on a tight budget you may want to consider an itinerary that has a departure port close to home. These cruises do not include airfare, so they are cheaper overall.

Budget Includes Ethical Tourism

What I aim to do with my tourist dollars (approx. A$100/port day) is distribute it over several small traders at a port to support local economy. I try to avoid spending in chain stores, instead aiming to spend money in local markets. I feel I am doing more value, distributing my tourist dollar by buying unique souvenirs that you can't find anywhere else, e.g. handmade or from local artists.

You may want to read a bit more on my blog post:

> www.julescruisecompanion.com.au/jules-experience-with-souvenirs

Book Early

If you want to do a particular itinerary, you need to book that cruise early before it sells out. Popular cruises such as Alaska with a short season and good cabins (balconies, suites) tend to book out quickly. You will always have the best selection of staterooms when the itineraries are first released. If you are adamant that you want a specific stateroom or itinerary you can take advantage of the best possible fare early. I would encourage booking 12 to 18 months out if you can, but definitely no later than 6 to 8 months out.

When it comes to getting the most cruise for your money, it pays to look at the whole package. That's because cruise lines are offering extra-value promotions, rather than price discounts, as incentives to book. These can include free beverage packages, gratuities, On-Board Credit (OBC), two-category upgrades, specialty dining and spa treatments or flights. In addition, some lines are offering reduced deposits and third/fourth passenger rates. The best way to compare offers or decide if you're getting a good deal is to look at the whole vacation (including airfare, on-board spending, shore excursions, insurance, pre- and post-cruise accommodation, etc.) and then put a dollar amount to the extra-value perks to see how much you're really saving or spending.

I have noticed that cruise lines seem to offer their best deals early. There rarely seems to be price drops on close-to-departure sailings. Booking early means putting a deposit on a stateroom and paying it off up to the final purchase date, which is usually 3 months before the sailing date.

Late Booking

Late bookings are bookings within 30 days of the sail date. These bookings often lose any bonuses such as On-Board Credit (OBC), paid gratuities or Beverage Packages (BP). This happened to me when I booked 28 days before sailing. I lost out on the included beverage package but gained two of the best barman friends in the world, (and many more friends on that cruise) and that was priceless. Keep looking at promotions especially on short cruises, as some companies may have policies where they do not discount sailings of five nights or longer within 30 days of departure.

Flexible

In reality no cruise line likes to sail with empty staterooms, so there may be some bargains to be found if you are flexible enough to cruise at short notice. Working full time, this option very rarely works for me. When I sail I just want to be on the ocean. I do not care what stateroom I am in. I know people have specific preferences for balconies, for fresh air, or whatever the case may be, but for me I just want to be at sea. If you are fussy and adamant, then be prepared to pay the price for what you want. Paying for an obstructed view outside stateroom may be a compromise.

If you just want to cruise and you are flexible with dates, itinerary and staterooms, just keep searching for a cruise bargain. In Australia, the Sunday newspaper travel supplement is packed with special offers. Signing up for email alerts from travel agents or cruise lines is another option. With more cruise lines coming down to Australian and New Zealand over the next few years, more last minutes bargains may appear.

Is the Priority the Ship or Itinerary?

Sometimes when you have chosen an itinerary, you may have a choice of ship. When you investigate a ship, do you want to sail on a brand new ship with newer features and testing glitches, or one that has already been broken in and dependable? Often when a cruise line launches a new ship, you may find discounts are available on existing older vessels thanks to decreasing demand.

If you choose a larger ship you will have more choice when it comes to restaurants and entertainment with standard itineraries, while smaller ships tend to be more upmarket and have more 'destination-rich itineraries. If you are choosing a smaller ship, they may have fewer itineraries, therefore the chance of last minute discounted bookings is lower.

Travel Agents

Use a travel agent to get a good deal on a great cruise as they can help you find the best deal. Travel agents know which promotions can be combined with others to get you an even better deal, and can point you toward the ship, sail date or cabin category with the greatest value.

If you are short on time, contact several travel agents to monitor the prices. Shop around and explore your options. Different cruise lines or travel companies or wholesalers may entice travellers with lucrative on-board perks, rather than lower prices. If a travel agent has a group departure booking it may have value-added on-board bonuses as well.

I am regularly seeing more deals appearing on my social media feed. You can start following the feeds from specific cruise lines or travel agents that operate in Australia. I have joined a few Facebook pages that have been set up by cruise fans who post hot deals they find. When you have cruised, you are automatically linked to the cruise line loyalty program. By visiting each cruise line's website you can sometimes find exclusive deals for loyalty club members.

Stateroom
For me, any stateroom is a good stateroom because it is on a ship. Some staterooms are a little more enjoyable than others. Once you have decided if you are a mid, forward or aft person then next thing to decide is which level of the ship you want to be.

In general, look at the placement of staterooms in relation to what is on the level above or below. Check the deck plan to see how close the stateroom is to the lift and stairwells. Check that you are not below the public spaces such as the pool, the nightclub, kids club or the dining rooms etc. A lot of long time cruisers will advise you being under these public spaces, may experience extra noise. In addition when choosing a stateroom, if family cabins (including connecting rooms), accessible rooms and suites are your priority, you should book these early as they tend to sell out first, regardless of destination.

If you are really on a tight budget, if a view of the sea isn't important or if you are planning to spend very little time in your stateroom, an inside stateroom is the best bet. You will find most cruise lines have aggressive prices for inside staterooms. However, a stateroom with an obstructed view is a reasonable alternative, as they are much cheaper than staterooms with sea views and balconies.

When choosing a stateroom, here are some things to consider:

Inside ~

- ☑ Cheaper,
- ☑ Lower in the middle,
- ☑ Better for motion sickness,
- ☑ Total blackout = Better sleep,
- ☑ Have standard amenities,
- ☑ May get engine vibrations or other noises,
- ☑ Some newer ships offer a 'Virtual Balcony'.

Ocean view ~

- ☑ Various window size, some are portholes while some are large,
- ☑ Similar size to an inside stateroom,
- ☑ Have standard amenities,
- ☑ Window covers let in some ambient light,
- ☑ May have an obstructed view or be on a promenade deck.

Balcony ~

- ☑ The view changes every moment of the day,
- ☑ No crowds,
- ☑ Staterooms are slightly bigger dimension,
- ☑ You can enjoy your own private space,
- ☑ Fresh air and smell of the ocean,
- ☑ More expensive,
- ☑ Staterooms at the stern of the ship may have more movement.

Mini Suite or Suite ~

- ☑ Most expensive,
- ☑ Have balconies,
- ☑ Have living areas, including a sofa, chairs, coffee table, mini-bar, sideboard and flat-screen TV, dining room, entertainment space and an extra bedroom,
- ☑ Additional facilities such as tea and coffee-making,
- ☑ Bathrooms with enhanced amenities,
- ☑ May include wine or welcome canapes,
- ☑ May come with reserved seating at shows or around the pool,
- ☑ May have exclusive dining venues,
- ☑ Many have a butler and/or concierge services,
- ☑ Will have priority check-in and tendering,
- ☑ Has private lounges, or separate lines, suite passengers get a quicker check-in process,
- ☑ May include all-inclusive beverage packages.

The important thing to consider when choosing a stateroom, is that the higher upfront expense is compensated by not having to spend on board.

Solo

If you are travelling alone, solo fares normally attract a 100% single supplement. If cruise lines cannot fill staterooms, some cruise lines may offer discounted single supplement rates as low as 25%. If you are thinking of cruising solo, you may want to book early if you want a single cabin.

Some cruise lines actually have solo studio staterooms with little or no additional single supplement fee. These solo studios are smaller staterooms with a full size bed and private bathroom. Ship designs incorporate solo staterooms with a communal lounge recreation space. Because limited ships have dedicated solo staterooms, your itinerary choice will be limited as well. Solo staterooms tend to book quickly so if this is your preference, book early. The price of a solo stateroom will be more than a 'per person' price in a standard shared stateroom, though lower than a standard stateroom with a Single Supplement Fee.

Though not specifically related to solo cruising you may be interested in reading a bonus blog from my travels in Jordan:

www.julescruisecompanion.com.au/solo-travel-in-jordan

Best Months for Value

When is the best time to book a cruise in Australia and get the best value for money? Do you get in early to get your dream itinerary to the South Pacific or around New Zealand in case it sells out, or do you bide your time and then pounce when a special deal is released at the last minute? In reality both approaches have their benefits. If you have specific preferences in terms of itinerary, time of year or which ship and type of cabin you want, then book early. Keep in mind that it's not only early or last-minute where you may pick up that bargain. If a cruise line is struggling to sell a particular sailing, promotional fares could be released at any time of the year.

In Australia the big selling periods are between the warmer months of October and April. With the 'wave period' of January and February, cruise lines have some of their best deals and increase effort for sales. During the months of June, July and August, travel companies launch itineraries for the following year with a release of a wide range of early-booking deals. These early-booking deals may be value added products, including On-Board Credit (OBC), cabin upgrades and free beverage or dining packages. In Australia, there is an initiative of CLIA, the Cruise Lines International Association, called Plan a Cruise Month which is usually during October.

In reality it is difficult to predict what a cruise line's pricing will be. With current technology, cruise lines have the ability to alter their fares on a daily or hourly basis. Pack 'n' Go offered on limited sail dates by P&O Australia and Carnival Cruise Line are specifically designed for people who have more flexibility and are happy to book sometimes with just a few days' notice. With these types of deals stateroom allocation will be completed 30 days before the sail date.

Loyalty Programs
The more you cruise with one company, the sooner you move through the loyalty program tiers. Each company offers different bonuses within each tier. Examples include receiving a bottle of free water, complimentary tote bag, discounted internet, upgraded toiletries, a free wash and fold service from the laundry, and invitations to functions to meet the senior crew. Some companies have offers that can escalate your progress through the tiers. For example, purchasing an itinerary over a certain amount of days, or six months before the sailing date, may afford you double the credited points, allowing you to

move through the tiers more quickly. As my personal cruise choices are governed by price and itinerary, and not specifically loyalty, I am on different levels with different companies.

> **All Hands on Deck:**
> - Google the cruise destinations
> - Write a bucket list then compare the destination and itineraries check out resource at the back of the book
> - Investigate different cruise lines.

4

Travel Trunk

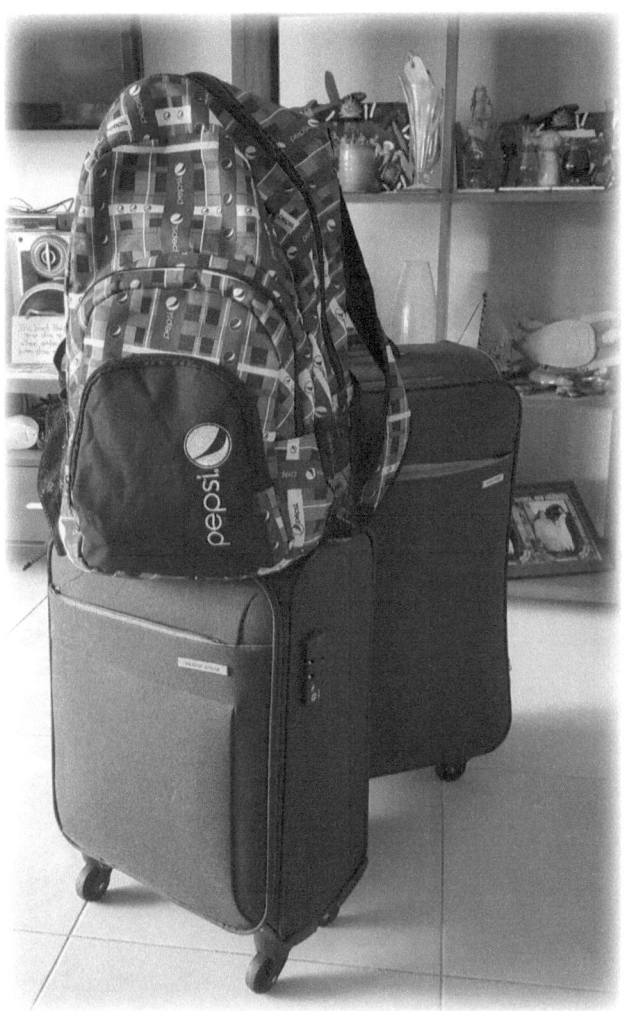

'For my part, I travel not to go anywhere, but to go. I travel for travel's sake. The great affairs is to move.'

~ Robert Louis Stevenson

If you get nothing out of this book, please do not be the person on the cruise who:

- ☑ Wears the hat with fake white spiked hair and a long plaited pigtail to hide your bald head,
- ☑ Wears a Bunnings wide-brimmed straw hat and a tank top, day and night for an entire week,
- ☑ Wears a white t-shirt with blue flowers every day,
- ☑ Wears clothing with the flag of his/her nation on shirts, shorts and pants.

Please, you look stupid, don't do it.

Have a trusted person look at your wardrobe and say yes or no to your clothing choices. No, two different patterns do not look good together, just because they are your favourite clothing items. One of my cardinal rules is, just because you like an item of clothing, does not mean it likes you!

Now that I have had my rant, I will talk to you about the dos and don'ts of carry-on luggage, personal item luggage, and checked luggage. Later in the chapter I will give you a cheat sheet list of basic items to pack. From the get go I will say *do not* take illegal drugs, weapons like firearms or knives, anything that could cause a fire, electric jugs, hairdryers, or candles etc. Please remember all my ideas are general in nature.

If you require more specific guidance about items such as medical assistance hardware, check out each cruise line's website, or contact me at: julie@julescruisecompanion.com.au, or check out my website: www.julescruisecompanion.com.au

What to do to Prepare for the Cruise

When you have decided on your cruise itinerary, it is time to start preparing the finer details such as how to prepare and what to pack. One of the most important steps to getting on your cruise is a visit to your Medical Officer, General Practitioner or specialised Travel Doctor. The Medical Officer will be able to give you advice if there are any unforeseen travel precautions, inoculations or medication risks. For example, if you have a medical condition, wear a Medic Alert Bracelet.

My standard safety tips regardless of ability is to carry emergency and doctor contact numbers with you at all times. Additional documents and information to take with you when travelling or cruising include:

- ☑ Doctors' names and contact information,
- ☑ A list of your current medications and dosages,
- ☑ Phone numbers and addresses of the local police and fire departments, hospitals and poison control of the destinations and country you are visiting,
- ☑ A list of food or drug allergies,
- ☑ Certified copies of legal papers (living will, advanced directives, power of attorney, etc.) or electronic copy,
- ☑ Names and contact information of friends and family members to call in case of an emergency,
- ☑ Insurance information (policy number, member name),
- ☑ DVT prophylaxis TED stockings,
- ☑ Sufficient medication for duration of the trip, and with some extra just in case your bags get lost.

If you are like me, you will have your suitcase always at the ready. If you are not like me, you might throw clothes into a suitcase over the weeks or days before your cruise. You might use a checklist or have a packing system, such as a space-saving packing technique, like rolling clothes or stuffing smalls into shoes. Whatever your system, as long as you are packing to go on a cruise, it is a good day. There is always the last minute, pack hours before you leave, technique. With this 'technique' comes the risk of not packing the right things.

Knowing what to take and what to leave behind are both equally important. Don't panic, if you leave something behind, you can buy a reasonably similar product while you are away! Sometimes you may just have to suck it up and pay for overpriced products to get you through, like warm socks, gloves or a warm hat.

If you are travelling to your cruise via an airline, unfortunately gone are the days of packing 15kg of everything into your carry-on. With the new 7kg restriction on carry-on luggage, some airlines are vigilant and weigh carry-on luggage at check-in. I cannot emphasise enough that you need to understand the luggage weight restrictions of airline carriers if you are travelling by plane to get to your cruise. Each airline will have varying regulations, especially the difference between domestic and international travel. My rule is pack checked luggage to the lowest airline checked luggage weight restriction. Some airline check-ins can be lenient, where others are strict, and every flight check-in is an adventure in itself. Over the years I have done the suitcase shuffle at a few airline check in counters. I have paid over 200 euro in excess baggage fees coming out of Russia because I was carrying 6kg of hardcopy cruise photos. I have worn my jacket with pockets laden with heavy items, then moved them into the carry-on luggage when I was in the terminal. You name it, I have most likely done it or seen it being done.

Carry-On Luggage is Your Backup Luggage
My 7kg carry-on is my backup suitcase. I always pack a change of clothes, multipurpose sleepwear, swimwear, a shawl, a light knit, a pair of shoes, jewellery, medication and travel toiletries. The reason for this is if your checked luggage gets lost in transit on the way to your cruise, at least you'll have some essentials with you to start. This gives you peace of mind as your luggage is found and then shipped to the next port or does not turn up at all. I met a passenger for a 3 week Trans-Pacific cruise, whose

luggage was lost in transit. She ended up borrowing clothes of other passengers. If you are a small clothing size you can get away with buying or borrowing clothes. If you wear a larger clothes size this is not as easy to achieve. Also, if your suitcase is delayed in being delivered to your stateroom, you'll have some essentials like a swimming costume or change of clothes for dinner. A shawl or pashmina can be used to dress up day clothes for evening wear, or can act as a blanket or a picnic rug. For gentlemen, pack a light jacket in your carry-on for evening wear.

In Your Personal Item
I cannot stress enough, keep all important documents on you in your handbag or backpack (personal item). Never pack necessary documents (such as a Driver's Licence or Passport, cruise documents or flight tickets, cameras and electronic items, medical records and medication) in checked luggage. Government issued photo ID will be required for every member of the travel party for the ship or flight check-in.

Once I packed my ESTA US Visa Waiver form in checked-luggage when I was leaving the US and narrowly was allowed to board the ship. I explained to the check-in clerk that I had entered the country at LAX airport with legal documentation, so there was a reasonable probability I could leave the country without showing my copy of the legal documentation. I was lucky they accepted my reasoning. I always travel with a passport but other forms of ID can be used such as an original birth certificate and photo ID for domestic cruises. An important thing to remember is that your identification has to be the same spelling as the reservation. So if your identification is in your maiden name and the booking is in your married name, sort it out long before you leave. You have to remember that some international travel requires visas or immunisations, so you need to carry those documents in your carry-on or personal item. In an emergency all your important documents need to be with you.

How to Choose a Suitcase (Aim for <23kg)

Everyone you speak to is going to have a different preference for the size and style of suitcase to use. Flying continually you will want to minimise the anxiety of excess baggage fees. I suggest using medium sized luggage as there will be less temptation to over pack. Regardless of your checked luggage allowance I always aim for less than a 23kg suitcase. 23kg is currently the standard Australian domestic checked luggage allowance. By the time you have purchased souvenirs and extra clothes along the way, there is all likelihood you will be close to your 30kg international checked luggage allowance.

One important thing to consider when purchasing your luggage is the weight of the luggage itself. The lighter the luggage the more you can pack in it. Consider purchasing the best quality, lightest suitcases you can afford. It will most likely last you longer, and may also have a long warranty or replacement offer. Currently I use 70 litre Hybrid luggage. A hybrid is a 3 in 1 combination between a traditional suitcase with a handle, a suitcase with wheels and straps that make it a backpack.

Check out my blog on how to choose the right luggage for you:

bit.ly/JCCPackingAAAAWhereDoIStart

Checked Luggage

The challenge for my travel is always having my checked luggage packed and underweight for any travel event. There are a few different packing techniques and you can find many of these on YouTube. Rolling clothes may save space, or there is currently a trend towards packing pockets. If you are an over-packer, my advice to you is pack, then unpack, and take half out.

If I have the capacity for 2 checked bags, I choose to pack an equal amount into each suitcase. If you are travelling with family like a spouse or children, divide everyone's clothes in two piles and pack half of everyone's clothes into each suitcase. This would go against the urge to put everyone's belongings into their own suitcase. The reason I suggest to spread all belongings over all suitcases, is that if one of the suitcases gets lost in transit, everyone will still have some clothes to wear.

I always aim for 18 to 20kg of checked luggage if I have a 23kg limit, or 25kg for a 30kg limit. This gives me leeway on check-in and allows for extra luggage weight on the return flight after shopping.

I cannot stress enough, *do not* put valuable items into the checked luggage. I encourage people to keep electronic copies on their smartphone of important documents and with an emergency contact back at home.

Mix & Match Clothes

I have several simple packing principles, all clothes have to be lightweight, block colours that mix-and-match, are interchangeable and multipurpose. As foundation items, opt for neutral base clothes and then use a splash of colour from scarves, necklaces or a necktie. When you are choosing which clothes to pack consider the weight of each item. If you have a choice between a pair of heavy wool slacks or a pair of lightweight cotton slacks, choose the lighter item. You will find they are more versatile in the long run. When I purchase clothes, I always have travel and packing in mind. I assess their weight and if they are too heavy I put them back on the rack.

The next principle to consider is layering your clothes. This technique serves a dual purpose, firstly for depth of layers with colours and texture and secondly for added warmth. When I talk about multipurpose clothing items I mean items of clothing that serve two or more purposes. By adhering to this principle, it will reduce the risk of over packing and being charged excess baggage fees. By taking fewer clothes it will also ease the stress of finding storage space in the stateroom. An example of a multipurpose item would be a neutral coloured t-shirt. It could be used through the day, at a beach, on an excursion, or used as a sleep shirt. I personally don't carry dedicated sleepwear, as they serve only one purpose, so for me, they are out.

My other guiding principle when choosing items of clothing to pack is to ask yourself how happy are you going to be looking at photos in years to come. I am not a fashionista, my core dress value is, if you can't see pubic hair, I am dressed.

But ask yourself, if you have paid money to go on a dream cruise to an exotic destination, why pack gardening clothes? You may look at your wardrobe and say to yourself, 'Which is my favourite dress?' Potentially it may not be the best choice for when you are travelling. You want to only take clothes that are comfortable and that look good on you.

Shoes

Always wear comfortable shoes that are tried and tested. There is one sure fire way to destroy your day and that is to wear uncomfortable shoes, new shoes, shoes that rub, or shoes with no support. If you are determined to take new shoes, break them in before you go. If your shoes are dirty, pack them in a shower cap or plastic bags. Packing your socks or intimate wear in your shoes helps keeps the shoe's shape, as well as saves space. Make an effort to take shoes that serve multiple purposes. Light weight shoes are a great idea. One of the best multipurpose clothing items I have seen in a long time was a pair of flip flops (thongs/pluggers) with a bottle opener concealed underneath. Those boys from Darwin Troy, Chopper, etc. are an ingenious mob.

Is There a Dress Code?

Every cruise line has a dress code, so do your homework before you start to pack. The cruise line website will tell you the number of formal nights, any theme nights, and a guide to general dress codes. If you love to dress up, you could save some packing room by renting a tux for example. Not everyone likes to dress up for formal nights, most people dress more informally with suits for men and cocktail outfits for women. You will find resort casual or smart casual is being embraced as evening wear, with men wearing slacks and buttoned shirts without jackets, and women in everything from nice dresses to skirts or slacks with cute tops. Jeans are also standard attire on many cruise ships in the main dining rooms. You will find specialty restaurants may require evening wear. Remember to always dress for your destination. I always pack seasonal costume wear when appropriate, such as Christmas, Halloween, Easter, pool party, 80s disco etc.

Dress for Your Itinerary

Simply put, some cruise destinations are more formal than others. Expect to pack more resort-casual wear if travelling to Europe (all regions) or Bermuda (Special alert, golf courses in Bermuda have strict dress codes). Other cruise itineraries, such as Hawaii, the Mexican Riviera, the Caribbean and Pacific Islands, are more casual than other destinations. As a cruise experience offers such diversity, don't forget to think about your in-port activities. Flip-flops/thongs/jandals are fine for a beach day, but you'll want more practical footwear for long days of sightseeing or active excursions like biking or hiking. If you are going to visit religious sites in the Middle East or some parts of Europe, you always need to dress in modest clothing that covers your shoulders and knees, even if it is hot. I always have a scarf or shawl on me for these occasions.

I cruised Transatlantic once and stayed on-board *unexpectedly* (Jules Code for didn't plan to, had a great time, so I stayed on board) and cruised Norway. Doing a cruise without preparing, it turned out to be an industrial case of layering. I have photos of me where I looked like I was a bag lady. This was not one of my most graceful outings.

When preparing to pack for your cruise, spend a little time researching the potential weather. On an Alaskan cruise, you may need clothing items ranging from swimwear for the hot tub, to full winter ski jackets and a knit hat all in one day.

On-Board Laundry

One of the challenges of packing light means you have to do laundry as you travel. Each stateroom has a small retractable clothes line in each bathroom. Different cruise lines have different services for doing laundry. Some have free self-service laundry rooms (very rare), while some have a small fee self-service laundry. There might be a fee-per-item laundry service (which can be expensive), or a fill-a-bag laundry service for a set price at some time during the cruise. You will become skilled at rolling as many of your clothes you can and fitting a lot into that fragile paper bag. With your name, stateroom and the deal flyer in the bag it goes to the on-board laundry to be returned in a few days washed and folded.

Complimentary laundry and pressing services are usually reserved for high-level loyalty passengers, or passengers in suites. When I am on board I try to balance my laundry costs by hand washing most of my clothes systematically and daily, using the laundry kit I carry with me. By taking a peg-less camping clothesline, suction cup hooks or S-hooks along with laundry detergent. I wash personal clothes each day and hang them in the bathroom or around the stateroom. It may be traumatic for my cruise buddy seeing my intimate wear hanging like oversized flags, suffice to say I have never run out of clean clothes.

There is a little known cruise phenomenon called *Laundry Rage*. I have been on ships were passengers have been sent off the ship for fighting over laundry. Clearly the worst comes out of holiday makers when there are long queues, laundry left in machines, or laundry touched by other passengers.

For a bonus check out my video of my laundry pack:

bit.ly/JCCMyLaundryPack

Taking the Toiletry Basics

Some cruise lines have reasonable basic toiletries on-board, such as soap and shampoo in your stateroom. Some toiletries are limited to pump bottles on the bathroom wall. If you desperately want your own toiletries, you will have to sacrifice packing space in your checked luggage. I don't know of a cruise line that will allow personal hair dryers to be brought on-board, and over the years I have seen confiscated items such as hair dryers, irons and hot water jugs. For me, I always have a travel toiletry bag packed all the times. I just top it up when I get back home and then it is all ready for the next cruise. My toiletry bag is one that has a hook to hang it in the bathroom, so I do not have to unpack it at all, everything is there, ready to use.

Taking the Household Basics

Most cruise staterooms have an alarm facility on the phone, so you do not need to pack an alarm clock. If you are using your smartphone as an alarm clock (or camera) just keep it on airplane mode so you are not charged roaming fees by your telecommunications carrier.

A random item I always pack when cruising is magnets. Magnets are handy as your stateroom door (and walls) are metal. I bring along a few cute magnets for three reasons. First, I put them on my stateroom door, as it helps identify and personalise your door as you walk down the generic corridor. It makes my door stand out so it is easy to find (late at night). Sometimes another cruiser will rearrange the magnets on the door each day, or sometimes someone will take their favourite one (it's fine, all part of the joy of cruising). Secondly, I use them to leave messages on the stateroom door for my cruise buddies or new friends. The third reason to bring magnets, is that I have no intention of ever taking them home, so they become souvenirs to give to people.

Other general household items to pack include over-the-counter meds, a portable battery pack, international power converter, camera memory cards, sunscreen, earplugs, and power strips to charge your electronics. Keep a plastic zip lock bag handy for liquids or wet items, or on the other hand, to keep belongings dry when doing water-sports.

Save Some Room in Your Suitcase

Collecting souvenirs is a standard part of cruising, so you may need some extra room in your luggage to bring them home. On one of my first trips on Norwegian Cruise Line (NCL) I needed extra luggage space so I purchased a foldable duffle bag. That yellow piece of NCL advertising goes with me every time I travel. It doesn't take up much space in the checked luggage, and there is the opportunity to fill it up and pay for extra checked luggage on the way home. Once I used it to carry fragile souvenir items home from Mexico. Going through security x-ray with this large carry-on was interesting – the two ceramic masks and the two 2 foot tall *Day of the Dead* figures cast uneven images on the x-ray machine. I was swabbed and searched at every security checkpoint.

Do Not Pack a Beach Towel

When you go on a cruise you do not need to pack a towel. Beach towels are either available free of charge or with a deposit on your Key Card. Wet towel receptacles are around the pool decks, gymnasium and spa area. If your holiday involves other land based activities that require a beach towel, buy a souvenir one when you get there.

All Hands on Deck:
- Look through your clothes to see what you would look good in on a ship
- Assess your empty suitcase weight – if it is heavy maybe it is time for an upgrade
- Stockpile travel size toiletries.

5

All Aboard

'Not all who those wander are lost.'

~ JRR Tolkien

To maximise your enjoyment on your cruise there are few things you need to consider before stepping on board the ship. In this chapter we will look at what to do in the weeks leading up to the cruise, what happens when you join the ship on the first day, and what happens when you are leaving the ship on the last day.

Before You Leave Home
In the months leading up to your cruise, start making a list of all the activities in your regular life you will need to deal with while you are away. Find a pet sitter, organise who will deal with the mail, bins and the garden. On the last few days before your cruise do the laundry and empty the refrigerator of perishable items.

It is important if you are travelling with a passport, that it is up to date. Most overseas travel requires your passport to be valid for 6 months after the date of travel. If you need to renew your passport or get a visa, organise that well in advance. Your travel agent or the country's embassy can give you guidance on the visa application process.

A few weeks before the cruise sail date you will complete the online booking process. This notifies the cruise line of your emergency contact details, any flight arrangements and your credit card details. When this stage is completed you will have online access to print off your boarding pass and your luggage tags. The luggage tags are printed on a standard A4 piece of paper with your name and stateroom number, as well folding instructions for you to follow. A tag printed in black and white is satisfactory.

Also during this time, investigate ground transport to and from the cruise terminal or to the airport. Depending on the embarkation port and the length of the trip, I vary my choices.

If my departure point is my local airport, I have someone drop me off or I will just catch a cab or Uber. For a short cruise from my home port I will drive to the port area and park in secured parking nearby that offers a shuttle service to the cruise terminal. If it is a longer trip usually involving international travel, I will purchase a shared shuttle ride or car hire service to the cruise terminal or airport.

I like to have a 'cruise countdown' in anticipation of an upcoming trip. There are a few apps available to create a cruise countdown, and you can post it online to share the excitement with friends. As the time draws closer some of those mundane chores like putting out the last rubbish bag become exciting.

On the day you leave, my mantra is Tickets, Passport, Money. Say it over to yourself as you are leaving the house, making sure you have valid government issued photo identification (ID). All cruise companies will require seeing this on check-in. Some ports require you to show a valid ID along with your cruise card to gain entry to the dock when reboarding the ship. I will continually stress to carry your ID on you at all times when visiting any foreign country.

Embarkation Day
Every cruise port is different. Some are purpose built, and some are makeshift huge tents. All cruise ports serve the one purpose, they are the gateway to your exciting cruise holiday.

When to Arrive at the Pier on Embarkation Day?
As it is a very busy day for the ship, with the disembarkation and embarkation of a few thousand new guests, some cruise lines will allocate you an arrival time to check in. I traditionally try to arrive around 11am to midday. The final time to board your cruise will depend on the ship's scheduled departure time, so refer to your cruise booking information. My rule of thumb is try to get to the ship for lunch.

I have recently heard one cruise line is considering charging an additional fee to allow you to be one of the first to board. When you have cruised before with a cruise line you often qualify for early boarding or fast track boarding without an additional charge.

I have only had an issue early boarding once where I was not allowed to proceed through the check-in process until my allotted time. So on that occasion I just went for a walk for an hour or so and then came back to the pier. That particular day was in Sydney. I chose, for a change of habit not to walk back to Circular Quay or over to the Opera House or into the Rocks. On this day I chose to walk around the shore line heading towards the Harbour Bridge. As I did so we noticed a nicely dressed Indian man taking selfies. So as I always do, I offered to take his photo for him for a different perspective. We got talking and now a few years later we are still Facebook friends. From this experience of not being allowed to board the ship early as I had planned, the Universe offered me an opportunity to meet this new friend.

As I have said, embarkation day is a very busy day. You arrive to the passenger drop-off area and will be guided to the luggage drop-off point. The port staff or stevedores will be helpful and ask if you have your important items such as documents, passport, boarding pass, money or medications. This is just a pleasant reminder that if you have put them into your checked luggage, you will not see it again until it is delivered to your stateroom later in the day. Then you will be asked to proceed into the cruise terminal following signs or staff directions towards the check-in desk.

As you enter the check-in stage, you will be asked to complete a health form. The health form varies from cruise line to cruise line, though its basic premise is to see if you have had a virus, cough, cold or norovirus in the preceding 48 hours. Helpful staff will guide you through the embarkation hall. I love the view of the check-in staff holding up a paddle to indicate they are at an available station for me to check-in. During the check-in process most cruise lines will take a digital photo of you to link it to your on-board Cruise Card. This is for additional security both on board and if you disembark over the cruise, so the security staff can see it is you entering or leaving the ship. You will be given your Cruise Card and a map of the ship before you move to a waiting area to be given further directions on where and when to board the ship.

How to Pay Your On-Board Account

Shipboard transactions are cashless transactions. Every purchase you make on-board any cruise line will be registered through your Cruise Card. On your Cruise Card will be printed a variety of things such as your name, the name of the ship or the cruise number and sail dates, your dining preference, your photo gallery portfolio number, your loyalty status, any packages you have purchased, and most importantly your Muster Station. Your Muster Station is your assigned meeting point in the unlikely event of an emergency.

All cruise lines will take your credit card details during the online check-in stage completed a few weeks before the cruise sail date. They may also scan a credit card on check-in on embarkation day. The credit card you entered on line and the one you present on embarkation day do not have to be the same credit card. Don't worry, when it actually comes time to pay for your on-board account at the end of the cruise, you can choose to pay with either cash or credit card. Always be vigilant with your on-board account, as occasionally random transactions appear that you may want to speak to the purser about.

If you want to control your spending and avoid credit card shock after the cruise, you can add cash to your Cruise Card at the pursers' desk. Some cruise lines debit the daily crew gratuity amount to your stateroom account each night. You can, if you wish, ask for that to be removed. This is something I do not recommend because if you do stop the automatic gratuity process, in my opinion, you best be willing to pay each individual crew member a gratuity at any time of service or at the end of the cruise.

As you are in the boarding process you will go through security scanning. This follows the same rules as any other transport security, removing all metal objects such as belts, money or phones from your pockets. As a frequent traveller, it still frustrates me that people complain about security checks. It is part of everyday life, so just get on with it. My advice is to prepare yourself, either don't wear a lot of metal in the first place or as you stand in line start getting yourself ready by taking the metal items off. Don't wait until you are at the head of the queue before you start thinking about what you need to do. Prepare by taking off your belt, and dig in your pockets for loose change and keys.

Each time you board or disembark the cruise ship security will scan your Cruise Card. My rule is, carry your Cruise Card on you at all times, and do not give it to anyone else to hold for you. I see continually people arguing with security, that my husband has the card or it is a domestic port and I don't need to take it. You are on a cruise ship with thousands of other people, security are there to keep you secure. It is the rule, just follow their instructions. Please, please, please, do not embarrass yourself by not carrying your Cruise Card.

Your First Time On Board Your Cruise Ship
You will find friendly crew are posted around the ship to meet and greet you and offer directions. As a turnaround day is very busy, housekeeping staff are sanitising staterooms so it can take up to mid-afternoon, around 1pm to gain access to your stateroom.

The room that you have been allocated is usually referred to as a stateroom or cabin. This is the perfect time before everyone is on-board for you to explore the ship and take some photos without having other passengers in the shot. This is also the time to have some food, either at the buffet or the main dining room. If you have packed your swimming costume in your carry-on, you can take advantage of the pool or hot tubs. You do not need to pack a towel, usually they will be available on the pool deck.

When the staterooms are open, you will be notified via the Public Address (PA) system, usually around 1pm. It is an exciting time when you head down to find your stateroom and to meet your stateroom steward for the first time. This is when you have an opportunity to ask for anything specific of your stateroom attendant. For example, I always like a fresh bucket of ice in my stateroom, as it serves two purposes. Firstly, I like to suck on ice (it's a ME thing) and secondly, the melted ice becomes water, so I have cold water available without having to pay for bottled water.

Another thing I choose to do at this time is take a photo of my stateroom number. I do this for two reasons, as a souvenir photo and for later, if I can't remember my stateroom number (for whatever reason, *Hello bartender*). I can show someone the photo so I can be directed to my floating home away from home.

Now that you are on-board, let me just say a few words about lift etiquette. I know, I can hear you say, 'What?' Believe me, you have to develop a special level of patience when waiting for a lift during a cruise. Such occasions include busy times like embarkation and disembarkation day, early on a port day and after the theatre shows of an evening. If you are heading to rendezvous, give yourself a little extra commute time. You are on holidays, so relax, and go find a bar until the busy period is over. You could always use the stairs, (yes, you could). There is always a solution on a cruise, you just need to be flexible.

What is in a Stateroom?
Each ship is designed and decorated very differently, with some basic guiding principles, your comfort and safety. Each stateroom contains your bed, a television, a telephone, a bathroom, wardrobe, draws, towels, some life jackets and information sheets. Most staterooms will also have a small bar fridge. When you first see a stateroom you may be concerned about the lack of storage. You will find some stateroom designs have hidden storage, for example if a table looks like a solid box, most likely the lid is movable and the body can be used for storage. Some foot rests of seats may also double as storage boxes. There is often additional space to store your empty suitcase under the bed.

Muster

To comply with International Convention for the Safety of Life at Sea, before any ship can leave a port with new passengers, they have to perform a muster or safety drill, so there is no need for Panic Stations. This drill varies from cruise line to cruise line, mimicking a nautical emergency. It allows passengers to familiarise themselves with the sound of the alarm and to learn the information they will need in order to stay safe in the unlikely event of an emergency. Just follow the instructions given over the Public Address (PA) system or by the crew. All shipboard services are stopped during this time. You have now been warned, so do not complain.

You are notified of the location of your personal muster station several ways. It is clearly marked on your Cruise Card, which you carry on you at all times. Another way is to check the sign on the back of your stateroom door. This sign will show you the fastest, most direct path to the muster station. Sometimes this may be through *Crew Only* areas.

Some musters are performed in public spaces such as the theatre, bars, casino or restaurants. Some musters are performed actually on deck at your assigned tender/lifeboat. The crew keep a record of all names assigned to each Muster Station so they can take a roll call and make sure everyone is accounted for.

During the muster drill you will hear the sound of the evacuation signal (7 short blasts, 1 long blast), at this time you will be told what to bring with you in the case of a real emergency (head covering, a jacket and any medications you may need). At this time the cruise line crew will also give you a demonstration of how to put on your life vest.

As indicated, each cruise line runs their musters slightly differently, some ask you to bring your life vest from the stateroom, and some don't. Just follow the directions of the crew on the day (yes, I can hear my German friends laughing). Please do not be the idiot who thinks they can miss the muster, it is mandatory. Your life or a member of you party's life could depend on it.

One element of cruising I have not gone in to depth on, is the marvellous crew who are going to make your cruise extra special. So as a bonus, here is a link to my blog posts:

Get to Know Your Crew:

> bit.ly/JCCGet2KnowTheCrewOnYourCruise

Amazing Service From the Crew:

> bit.ly/JCCAmazingServiceFromTheCrew

Disembarkation Day

Most cruise lines have roughly the same process. There are some mild variations, but the principles of disembarkation (turnaround day) remain the same – get thousands of old passengers off, and get thousands of new passengers on.

In preparation for disembarkation the cruise line has to be notified of your travel plans when leaving the ship. This can be done at time of booking, during your online check-in process, or with the pursers' office while on-board. If you have a flight to catch, my rule is always book it for after 12 midday. It reduces the stress on disembarkation day.

You are notified that disembarkation day is approaching. You are given the instructions in writing about the process and several colour coded luggage tags for your luggage. If you require more colour coded disembarkation luggage tags they are available at the pursers' office. The written information will have instructions about what time the luggage needs to be outside your cabin for collection by the crew, where your meeting place is to wait for your disembarkation announcement, and you are given your allocated time slot for disembarking.

This process is tried and true and works. I see people trying to take all their own luggage off the ship on the morning of disembarkation and it is chaos. The other thing I have witnessed is people complaining about the process – just relax and breathe! The crew want you off the ship, and they are not doing anything deliberately to keep you there. You will be allowed off when the ship is cleared by the local authorities.

The Day Before Disembarkation Packing
I choose to pack in the morning on the last full cruise day. For me I am not going to spend my afternoon and evening in my stateroom squashing the washing into the suitcase. I want to spend my last afternoon and evening of a cruise having a great time socialising and partying with my new friends. The night before disembarkation day you need have your luggage ready to be out in the corridor near your stateroom by the designated time. The crew will take it and it will reappear the next day on the dock ready for collection. Some people choose to take all their luggage off on disembarkation. This is a very bad idea, there is limited lift access and hauling large suitcases around a crowded ship is dangerous.

The Morning of Disembarkation
The aim is to have everyone out of staterooms by 8am so that the stateroom stewards can disinfect and turn the staterooms around for the oncoming passengers by 1pm. You can either leave your remaining carry-on luggage in the stateroom until you have finished breakfast and then return to your stateroom and remove it before 8am, or take all your remaining carry-on luggage with you to breakfast. By doing this your stateroom steward can start their very busy day turning the rooms around. You will be notified in your daily cruise newsletter of the breakfast venues. Breakfast will be served in several locations from early in the morning around 6am until about 9am. Room service is never available on a disembarkation day.

Customs and Immigration
Declare everything to Customs and Immigration. In all my years of travel I have only had one issue with customs and one issue with immigration. When purchasing souvenirs, especially wood products from island nations, be conscious of Australian Biosecurity regulations, as that cheap wood souvenir may end up costing a few extra dollars. My Customs experience came after the Papua New Guinea cruise, I had deliberately purchased 4 or 5 big tribal wooden items over the two weeks, so I knew I had to declare them. The friendly quarantine inspection man was very thorough, he suspected borers in 3 of

the 5 items and said they would need to be treated. I asked how much that would cost and he said AUD $100. I asked if that was per item, and he said it was for the three. As I could I get them all done for the one price, I chose to have all 5 items treated. He gave me a receipt for my items and the transaction, along with the information sheet about the location of the treatment, the type of treatment and the estimated time the items would be returned to me. However when leaving New Zealand I had a lot of wood items to declare, upon inspection they were deemed ok and I was allowed to pass with them.

My immigration experience was very early in my travelling career around 1990. I was heading back into England at the end of my 2 year Work Visa, to be with my then partner and hopefully apply to a nursing school in England. I landed at Heathrow at 6am after the long haul flight to be greeted by a female Immigration Official of Indian heritage. I was dressed in a very comfortable, bright, multi-coloured psychedelic t-shirt with a spiral of teddy bears on the front. I loved that shirt. Clearly, after a brief explanation of why I was trying to enter the UK, 'something' raised the suspicions of this officer, so she flicked through her ring binder over and over hoping to spot my name on the banned list. Time passed and all the passengers from my flight had been processed and other flights were arriving to be processed in the immigration hall and I was still waiting at the counter. After searching through this ring binder over and over and over, she told me to sit back on the available chairs and she left the counter area. I waited and watched 2 or 3 more flights enter and leave the immigration hall. Eventually, she came back to her station and called me over. She said, 'We have spoken to your partner, he is an Englishman with Australian Residency so you are allowed to enter the UK.' That was a lesson on the power that one individual has to make an assessment based on a brief conversation and personal appearance. It could have changed my destiny. I went on to marry my partner, go to nursing school in England and have a wonderful son. From that day on I have always dressed conservatively when I travel and only told immigration about my holiday plans and not my life plans.

5. All Aboard

All Hands on Deck:
- Check out some of my souvenir stories: bit.ly/JCCExperienceWithSourvenirs
- For a cruise countdown checklist check out an additional bonus offer at the back of the book.

6

Cruise Card

'Ships are the nearest things to dreams that hands have ever made.'
~ Robert N. Rose

To maximise your enjoyment on your cruise, there are few things you need to consider before stepping on board the ship. In this chapter we will look at on-board spending, the different types of packages available, shore excursions, and discuss ways to save money, maximise your budget and have the best experience.

Cruises need to be completely paid off around 3 months before the sail day. This is an exciting time as you are starting to live your cruise experience. Now you can start budgeting and saving for any other expenses such as getting to the ship, drinks money and excursions.

Some people wonder about the cost of extra activities and if they can afford them. What you need to do is decide on your *must-do* activities and spend money on achieving them. My tip to avoid you missing out on your preferred *must-do* activities is look on the cruise website of your cruise line and to book and pay for packages before you leave. You can do this online up to 2 to 3 days before sailing. Packages sold online before your set sail day are often discounted. What I suggest is to prioritise your spending money. You can save money by not going to the casino and definitely not going to the art auction.

Beverage Packages

There are a few advantages to purchasing a beverage package. You don't need to spend your cruise worrying about if you can afford a drink, and you just get on with enjoying yourself and participating in activities. You are on holidays, and you don't have to drive anywhere. It is your time to enjoy the social life on the high seas.

A beverage package is an inclusive drinks product, but read the fine print as there are always restrictions. In reality it is a brilliant social experience which allows you to maximise your participation on board. I am frequently asked if a drinks package is good value. If you are a drinker, the answer is yes. Compared with buying drinks individually, you won't experience the same 'bill shock' at the end of the cruise. An added bonus is befriending the lovely bartenders, as they make your cruise even **more** enjoyable.

If you are a non-drinker, the non-alcoholic beverage packages are just as good value. You can save a bit of money on drinks if you are invited to on-board functions, such a captain's meet and greet, or cruise loyalty function. You will often be served with a drink on arrival, or there may be free drinks for a period of time during these functions. Another way to get a free drink it to attend the art auctions. Though keep in mind if you bid on a piece of art, a free drink may end up costing you a bit of money. For a moderate fee, wine or cocktail tasting demonstrations may be another way to save a little money. If you get called on stage during a culinary or cocktail demonstration you may be lucky enough to try a few nips of something on display.

Photo Packages

Some people make a fuss about having professional photos taken on a cruise. Cruise line photographers are professionals, so they are good at making you look good. You may notice they give you advice about how to stand, where to put your hands, which direction to face, to hold a prop, etc. You may find this boring or uncomfortable, but in reality, they are making you look good. After so many cruises, I have built my own repertoire of poses and often find that most photographers will enjoy the variety and playfulness. Another thing I choose to do is carry my own props. It is usually something small like a fan, tiara, plastic blow up palm tree or a pink flamingo or toucan. If, like me, you like having professional photos taken, it can be wise to enquire about the ways of saving some money. If you are travelling in a large group this may be an economical way to capture additional cruise memories.

Dining and Bars

There are several complimentary dining options on-board including formal and informal atmospheres. Some cruise lines have formal dining times, where others have a more flexible walk in or reservation methods. I do have a few rules when attending the main dining room. The first is, don't be late for your allocated time. It delays the service and it is plain rude. Secondly, you may be on a shared table, which is a larger table where up to 10 diners can be served. This is a great opportunity to meet your fellow passengers, and there are few different ways this system works. There is the system where you are allocated the same table each night, so you share the experience with the same guests each night. Then there is the system where you are randomly allocated a table with different diners each night. Both systems have their merit, and both have their pitfalls.

Specialty restaurants and Chef Table dining experiences are becoming more and more common with most cruise lines. If you are celebrating a special occasion, it is a wonderful treat. There will be a reasonable cover charge from $15 or more. Packages are available for pre-purchase or to purchase on-board. You will normally have to make reservation as early as possible as prime times fill up quickly. Depending on the day you could walk up and be seated, but most times you will need a reservation. If you are not able to make an evening reservation, a lunch time reservation will be just as enjoyable. Dress codes for speciality restaurants may be stricter than the main dining room, so pack at least one nicer outfit.

As an extra bonus, here is a full blog on dining on board a cruise:

bit.ly/JCCWhat2ExpectFromDiningOnACruise

Internet
Welcome to the modern age. Congratulations if you can do without internet for 1 to 30 days, but that is not me. My record on a cruise ship was 3 days without internet. Yes, it is a First World problem and I am addicted. With the use of smartphones for photography, banking, communication, email, Facebook, and Instagram etc., cutting yourself off from the internet can be very difficult. Internet services on cruise ships can guarantee two things, it is expensive and it is slow. This is slowly changing, and will be demand driven. Prepaid internet packages can reasonably meet most needs. Internet in public spaces such as the atrium or library is often better quality than in your stateroom. Prepaid unlimited packages can give reasonable access over the entire cruise. Remember to read the package fine print, as often only one device can be online at any one time.

Other price points of internet packages may offer multiple device options, and there are often 24 hour internet access options for around US$30 a day on some cruise lines. Some cruise lines may also offer a discounted unlimited option near the end of a longer cruise. Like any purchase, evaluate the benefit to you, budget for it, and just do it. When you cruise with the same cruise line often, some of the loyalty bonuses may include a small amount of free limited time or discounted internet access. I cannot stress enough to put your phone on Flight Mode to avoid bill shock.

Shore Excursions

In this section, I aim to cover all the basic concepts of shore excursions, such as choosing an excursion, the types of excursions, what to do and what not to do. Before I start, there are a few things I want to point out. One thing to be aware of when cruising is that no port is guaranteed. Due to circumstances out of anyone's control, such as weather or safety issue, a port visit could be cancelled. Relax, and don't complain. You are on holidays and the cruise line will put on activities on board to keep you occupied. When leaving the ship at any time, *do not* under any circumstances take food or drinks (except sealed bottled water) off the ship. Most countries have strict bio-quarantine laws, and you could be prosecuted if you are found in breach of these laws.

Here is an added bonus of my blog on my experiences with shore excursions:

bit.ly/JCCExperienceWithShoreExcursions

Choosing an Excursion

Should you do an excursion with the cruise line, an independent contractor, or by yourself? You can find independent tourist providers online before you travel, or find them touting their services on every pier. The answer is, do whichever you want, but remember there are always consequences. Allow me to explain.

Shore excursions with the cruise line (involving third party operators) come with some positives, such as a great overview of the location, registered tour guides, regulated industry standards, return transport to the ship, and an assurance that the ship will not leave port without you. Some negatives of purchasing shore excursions with the cruise line, is they can appear expensive, regimented, and they guide you to their preferred locations. They can also be tiring, especially on consecutive shore days. Let's be honest – cruising is a business and they are there to make a profit and so are the local tour operators.

On the cruise line's website and on board the ship, there is information about all the shore excursions that will be available on your itinerary. Along with the title of the excursion will be a brief description, the cost, inclusions and exclusions, the activity level, and any restrictions noted in both writing and in an icon legend. An inclusion may be lunch or a drink of the local beverage, while exclusions may include the company not providing lunch or towels or drinking water. In the case of exclusions, it is your responsibility to provide those items. If you like the look of an excursion, book it online before you go, you may get a discount. The only disadvantage is you have to pay for it when you book. The advantage is, if it's a popular excursion, you are more likely going to be on that excursion.

Be vigilant and pay attention to the activity level of each excursion, these may have a description such as low, medium or high. Low indicates not much walking, a few stairs, and is a fairly passive activity. A medium level activity may involve more walking, or rough surfaces. A high activity level indicates a very active activity that may involve zip lining, riding in an ATV, or horseback riding etc. Some restrictions on excursions may include mobility restrictions, that are not suitable for wheelchairs or children, or weight restrictions, for example on Segways or ATV or Zip Lines. The rule is, read the descriptions and the fine print before paying for the excursion.

When you have chosen your excursion and paid, you will be issued a ticket. On the ticket will be the excursion name and code, your name, the meeting point and meeting time. If pre-purchasing before you board, your shore excursion ticket will be sent to your stateroom. If booking at the Shore Excursion Desk on-board, you will be issued with a ticket at the time. Read the ticket carefully and check the details are correct. It is your responsibility to bring that shore excursion ticket with you on the day of the excursion to the designated meeting point.

Like everything in life, there are no guarantees. On the days before the excursion or the day of the excursion, some excursions may be cancelled due to bad weather or lack of participants. In this instance, you will be notified and your money reimbursed to your on board account. You may then choose to do a different excursion or do your own thing while ashore.

The advantage of purchasing an independent tour operator is they may be cheaper and appear more flexible. The negative aspect, however, is they may not be regulated or have insurance, and they might use a vehicle that is not roadworthy. But most importantly, they might not get you back to the ship on time. So what appeared like a good deal at the beginning of the day may turn into an expensive lesson.

If you choose not to do a ship organised shore excursion, you can still have fun exploring your holiday destination. On every pier there will be local tour operators offering their services. It can be intimidating, running the gauntlet of touting men on a foreign shore. Don't make eye contact, just be polite and say no.

Choosing a local operator at the pier may appear cheaper in the first instance, but there may be hidden costs. At the end of the day you don't want to say, I saved a few bucks doing an excursion but it cost me a fortune to re-join the ship because I missed the departure time. So you remember your cheap excursion could cost time, energy, enjoyment and money.

Cardinal Rules for Shore Excursions

Dress appropriately
- ☑ Respect local customs,
- ☑ Dress for the activity and the weather,
- ☑ Wear comfortable shoes,
- ☑ Avoid wearing valuable jewellery.

Bring your government issued photo identification
- ☑ A minimum of a driver's license on you at all times,
- ☑ A passport,
- ☑ On-board Cruise Card plus shore excursion ticket.

Carry cash – Always carry a small amount of cash (about A$100) or the equivalent in local currency, preferably in small denominations, along with a credit card.

Do not forget essentials
- ☑ Sunscreen,
- ☑ Sunglasses,
- ☑ Headache or essential meds,
- ☑ Water bottle,
- ☑ A hat,
- ☑ A day pack.

Do not show up late – turn up on time. Go to the bathroom before the gathering time. Have all your party with you ready to leave for the excursion meeting point.

Research your port – get an insight into the local culture, dress standards, etc.

Listen to the safety briefing – If you are required to, attend a safety briefing that has rules to prevent injury, or you may lose out on some insider tips.

Read the fine print – inclusions or exclusions of the shore excursion.
- ☑ Meeting time and location,
- ☑ The length of the excursion,
- ☑ Activity level.

Do not overdo the activities – Don't push yourself to the point you get dehydrated, hurt or injured on a shore excursion.

DO NOT lose track of time – It's five o'clock somewhere. When you are relaxing (or overindulging) at shore bar, the ship will leave without you.

If you are wandering on your own time, make sure your watch is on the ship's time. Remember, you need to add an additional time buffer so you are not on the last tender.

For a more detailed overview of my cardinal rules to shore excursion check out:

www.julescruisecompanion.com.au/cardinal-rules-for-shore-excursions

I cannot stress enough, what people may not realise is if you take a shore excursion that is *not* linked to the cruise line, they are *not* obliged to wait for you.

People often ask me if I've seen people left behind on ports? Yes – on an Alaskan cruise, the captain left people behind at two different ports, Juneau and Ketchikan. Being left behind in Alaska is very expensive and there are limited flights and boat access. If I was going to be left behind it would be better in somewhere like Victoria, British Columbia because Seattle is just a short plane ride over the mountains to collect my luggage the next day.

There are YouTube clips of passengers being left behind on cruises, it may be uncomfortable to watch, some are hilarious. You have to remember you are on your holiday and so are thousands of other passengers, it is expensive to delay a departure as the cruise line who has to pay additional port fees all for a few passengers. If you do miss the ship there are port agents who will assist people at your own expense. The take home rule is, *don't* be late back to the boat.

Port Access
All ports vary with the quality of their facilities. At some ports, cruise ships berth at a pier that are purpose-built passenger terminals, and other ships berth at piers that are industrial working ports. When I first started cruising I used to feel negative about an industrial berth. Now after travelling so much, I have seen how vital tanker ships and container terminals are to the life blood of some nations, and I am in awe. The engineering of a container port is like poetry of economics. It is the most beautiful thing I have seen.

Some ports have no capacity for ships to dock at a pier, so passengers are moved ashore by smaller boats or tenders. The tendering process can be by the ship's own tenders or by hired independent third party tenders. The tender process is like a major military action. Passengers that have shore excursions meet at their designated meeting points, and are escorted to the tenders when available. Passengers leaving the ship independently will be given instructions on how the tender disembarkation will be managed. This can happen in a few different ways, such as going to a designated point to receive a ticket that will be called when it is their turn to disembark, or standing and waiting in a line until the next available vessel. An important thing to remember is tenders are not wheelchair accessible for shore excursions. The flip side of this is, the crew are specially trained to deal with passengers with accessibility issues during an evacuation for emergency procedures. This disability accessibility is not to be confused with general accessibility during a shore excursion.

All Hands on Deck:
- Check out a cruise line's packages on line or ask a travel agent
- Look at the types of excursions offered by each cruise line in a brochure from a travel agent.

7

Salty Sea Dog

'There is NOTHING – absolutely nothing – half so much worth
doing as simply messing about in boats.'

~ Kenneth Grahame, from Wind in the Willows

Now that we are on our cruise, let's talk about different activities. What do you do on a sea day or even a rainy day? It is important not to confuse a sea day with a rainy day while cruising. It is the smallest, yet most significant difference that will leave you stunned. A sea day will only ever be a sea day. Whereas a rainy day can be any day – a sea day or a port day.

What to do on a Sea Day

I absolutely love sea days when cruising. The longer the cruise, the more sea days there are. There is so much to do on-board, and you can do as much or as little as you like. Organised activities start from around 6am and continue until after midnight. For me, I find the slower my start to a sea day (natural wake up, lazy shower and dress, meander to breakfast) it sets me up for an amazing time on the high sea.

Exercise

If you have some extra energy you can go to the gym or fitness centre on board. Yes, I said it, exercise. With world class state-of-the-art equipment, most ships have a fitness centre with ocean views, and some may have views of the decks or pool areas. Different cruise companies have a variety of exercise programs available, such as walking, resistance training, swimming, indoor rock climbing, waveriders, zip-lining, Zumba, mini-golf, basketball and more. If the idea of the gym is not exciting to you, you can still get plenty of exercise without going to formal classes. It's easy to get your cardio workout in by just walking around the ship or up the stairs when you can. Enjoy your day at sea!

Pool

One of the main attractions of a cruise is the pool. Spend a sea day on the pool deck, sunbathing and relaxing. There will be a hot tub, and lounge chairs or cabanas for your leisure. Some ships have wave pools for you to surf, and water parks and wading pool for kids. There are also some cruise ships with water slides that circumnavigate the whole ship. Adult-only solariums on some ships could be your sanctuary, some are open air where others may have retractable roofs.

Activities & Lectures

Your daily cruise newsletter will give you the running schedule for the activities of the day. Some cruise lines have guest speakers or guest dance instructors. There may even be a passenger choir you can join, or competitions at the casino (remember to gamble responsibly). On a few cruises I had the opportunity to take Spanish and Malay lessons, taught by a crew member. I have also attended Learn to Cook classes, culinary demonstrations and even made hats and fascinators taught by a guest milliner. No cruise is complete without a couple of rounds of trivia through the day, for no reward except the glory. Whether it be scrapbooking, jewellery making, computer lessons or digital photography classes, every cruise line will have something different for you to do.

Movies & Shows

You can while away the day watching a midday movie, or a dive-in movie while in the pool. You will find matinee performances, game shows, or karaoke, or you could even enter the hairy man competition (a cringe worthy display, where a small group of passengers volunteer to allow fellow passengers to vote on their unique holiday hairy bodies). Some cruise lines will have musical performances or culinary displays in public areas like the atrium or promenading characters or ship wide scavenger hunts. Look out for shows and demonstrations in the daily shipboard newsletter.

Ship Tour

Fascinating behind-the-scenes galley tours are offered on some ships. Very few cruise lines offer behind the scenes tours for free, and some cruise lines may offer a tour as part of the loyalty program. Most will charge a nominal fee on sea days for these interesting tours. It is enlightening to see the busy staff in action in the huge, industrial kitchen. It brings you a greater understanding about the logistic of a cruise ship when you see the inner-workings. On these tours you will discover fun facts, for example, the number of plates of food served at a service, and how many kilos of a produce is used. Sometimes there may be a sample of food and drink during the tour. A laundry tour will also leave you amazed. It is a testament to the hardworking crew that so much quality service is delivered on a daily basis, rain, hail or shine.

Eat

There is never an issue with the variety of food on offer on a cruise, so a sea day could be a good opportunity to try something different. Start your day with a quiet private breakfast in your stateroom. Some cruise lines may have a speciality day like sushi, Indian, Italian, or Mexican served at the buffet. There might also be a High Tea offered in a specialty restaurant or main dining room, usually for a nominal fee. Some cruises may have a chocolate day from breakfast to evening meal (warning: may include chocolate). During a sea day, you may decide to have lunch in a specialty restaurant and enjoy the experience of dining in top class restaurant. You may find there is a discount for lunch, just ask.

Spa Visit

A sea day can be an ideal day for pampering. Options may include a massage (Hot-Stone or Bamboo), facial, mani-pedi, Botox injections, teeth-whitening treatments, fancy shaves for men, teen treatments, couples mud baths, circulation treatments, saunas, steam rooms and heated relaxation chairs, sometimes with an ocean view.

Drinks Day

A nice day at sea may be a liquid day. You could start your 'liquid day' with a spicy Bloody Mary or her cousin Maria (tequila), followed by a full liquid diet with endless beer buckets or fruity cocktails from any bar. You can be more refined at lunch or dinner with a glass of wine. Remember to drink responsibly.

Bingo

No sea day would be complete without a game of bingo. With the dabber in hand or an electronic tablet, there is always an electrifying atmosphere in the room. Though bingo is always better on the last day of a cruise with the big jackpot, any day is a good day to dream about shouting 'Bingo!'

What to do on a Rainy Day

Now that we have covered ten things to do on a sea day, we will look at what to do on a rainy day. I mentioned earlier the difference between a sea day and rainy day. Remember that a rainy day could be either a sea day or a port day. So let's throw ourselves into a few suggestions for a rainy day.

Spa Day. A rainy day spent being pampered in the spa will relax and calm you. You could indulge in a hot stone treatment, seaweed facial, couple's massage, or circulation treatments. Relax in a sauna or hot-tub, and the rainy day will vanish to a distant memory. Often on a port day spa and salon services are at a discounted rate.

Reading Day. Some cruise ships have well stocked libraries with easy chairs, some have a games room with board games, or you could find a quiet corner to read your own book or kindle.

Singing Day. Sing the rain away at Karaoke. If you are not brave enough to perform, it is very rewarding being in the audience. You might find some of your fellow passengers to be hiding an amazing talent (or not). My go-to karaoke songs are Khe Sanh (Cold Chiesel) and My Way (Frank Sinatra).

Movie Day. A movie day on the high seas can make you forget about the rain. Some cruise lines have free movies available on your cabin TV, some have them at set times in the main theatre, or a dedicated movie theatre.

Arcade Day. Anyone for a little game of foosball? Arcades are not only for the kids. You will definitely see some different faces in the games room, young and old. Arcade tokens or credit will be credited to your shop board account as you play shootem up, or excel at car or motorbike rides.

Stateroom Day. You have paid for that stateroom, so enjoy it as much as you like. Whether an inside or ocean view, a balcony or a suite, start the day with room service breakfast and enjoy the space you are in. Being on the high sea, rain can seem different. You can look out at the ocean and see a rain cloud dropping rain in the distance, while the boat is under blue skies. It is amazing. Rain at sea can be its own form of meditation. Breathe in, breathe out.

Pool Deck Day (Yes, in the rain). For safety reasons, the deck chairs around the pool deck are usually cleared away on a rainy day, but you will still be able to find a place to sit in a covered area. Sit and enjoy the view of the pool deck, maybe watch a movie on the TV screen or just enjoy a dose of people watching.

Workout Day. Ouch! Yes, exercise, I said it again. It (most likely) won't kill you. It's a rainy day, so try something different. You can stay out of the rain but work up a sweat being active. Some ships have their gym with an ocean view, so you can still watch the rain while on your calorific tour of the high seas.

Photo day. I take photos of everything, so when I get home I have a lot of amazing images, unique to that ship. I like to compile these into a glossy A4 coffee table photo book. I remember while exploring on one ship, I saw some of the wall art reproductions that looked really familiar. It occurred to me that I had decorated one of my houses in the 90s with the same prints. Spend your rainy day sorting through and editing your photos.

Ship Day. On a rainy port day, stay on board and explore the ship. No two cruise ships are the same, each have their own magic that most passengers would simply walk past. Even if I have been on a ship before I always like to wander and explore all the public spaces. Be sure to stay out of Crew Only areas and enjoy your day.

All Hands on Deck:
- Talk to your travel buddy about what they want to see and do. Devise a plan. It is OK not to do everything together.
- Practise your trivia skills
- Sharpen your card skills or Karaoke.

8
A Burly Chum

'Attitude is the difference between an ordeal and adventure.'
~ Bob Bitchin

The more I talk about cruising, the more ridiculous excuses I hear not to cruise. In reality it may be a good thing that those people choose not to cruise, as I wholly expect they would be miserable people to be around on the open ocean. Someone once said to me that they didn't want to be in a small room with their snoring partner, as it would drive them mad. I asked if they slept in the same room at home, and if their partner snores at home. The answer was yes to both, to which I said that being on ship will be no different! People say, my partner/cruise buddy doesn't want to do the activities I want to do. Well I say, that's fantastic! It gives you both a chance to do other things and to meet other people. You can catch up with your cruise partner later in the day and share stories.

While this chapter is not a definitive list of how to be a good cruise buddy, it does include a summary and list of ideas that could make your cruise more enjoyable. With a positive attitude and a willingness to get out of your comfort zone, practice mindfulness and be open for personal growth and new experiences. Cruising is your ticket to seeing the world.

Travelling with other people is often a challenge, so to ease tensions, clear, open and honest communication is important. There are morning people and there are night owls. Some will want to go to every museum or gallery, others may not. It's important to find a balance. One strategy to address this is to take turns at choosing the daily itinerary, or where to eat a meal, for example. Often when you do something you hadn't previously considered, you may learn a little more about yourself. I refer to my cruising motto, *Open Heart, Open Mind*.

An important thing to consider when travelling with other people is being punctual. If you have decided on an activity and it is not one you are particularly interested in, and you have discussed options and decided on a meeting time, be respectful and show up on time. There will come another time on the trip where it is your activity that has been decided upon and you will expect the other members of the party to be respectful to you.

When travelling with other people, conflict may come from differences in perspective. For example, everyone may have their own strategy about getting to a location, and these differences may cause tension. An important part of learning about yourself is that you do not always have to be right. It could turn out that taking the slow route or a different route may lead to more memorable adventures. From my experience, some of the best travel adventures evolved organically with little or no preparation. My plans to Macedonia changed unexpectedly, with the new short notice plans turning out amazingly. Before I went on my second trip to Jordan I said it was either going to be either the worst experience or the best experience, but I am going to do it anyway. It turned out to be more memorable than any amount of preparation could have anticipated. There is the saying, it is not about the destination it is about the journey. My advice is to take a deep breath, take a step and enjoy the journey.

Travelling with others may reveal that you are not synchronised with sleeping patterns or mealtime patterns. None of these are an issue. There are no rules to say everyone has to do the same things all the time. If you are a morning person and your travel buddy isn't, be proactive and get your clothes ready the night before. Leave them in the bathroom so you won't disturb them when you get up and leave in the morning. Similarly, if you're going to come in late at night, leave your sleep clothes in the bathroom before you go out, so that you can prepare for bed without disturbing your sleeping roommate.

If your roommate is a snorer, be proactive and take some ear plugs or have some relaxation music to play while you are going to sleep. There is all likelihood that it turns out you too have an annoying habit that will not excite your roommate, so a large dose of tolerance will serve you both.

Sharing a stateroom with a cruise buddy can be less stressful and you can reduce conflict by allocating sides or space in the stateroom. For example, split the wardrobes drawers or shelves to have a side each. Aim to keep a neutral space for shared items such as brochures, water, power charge cords, etc. Staying tidy while sharing a confined space like a stateroom can ease some tensions. Being disciplined with staying tidy in the stateroom is not to be confused with being obsessive.

I have been in a situation where the person I was travelling with did not like doing laundry. After a few weeks, I observed a pattern of behaviour where if I offered to do the laundry they would take me up on the offer, but the offer was never reciprocated. I allowed this behaviour to continue because I was feeling sufficiently recompensed with not having to contribute to paying for the duty free liquor. Though there was no formal agreement, the issue passed uncontested thanks to the Opal Nera.

To be a good travel buddy you do not have to be together all of the time. You will meet more people along the way to share experiences. One of the most amazing things about travelling is the amount of interesting travellers you meet. Sometimes you may have the opportunity to invite other people into your party for a day, or you may be able to join another party for the day. While this may not be possible all the time, it is OK to split from your travel buddy for a period of time. It is a great way to learn that you can gain a new perspective by being around other people. You can regroup and refocus yourself and then later in the day get back together.

Sometimes expectations before the cruise may not have been specified or were misunderstood. I had a situation where I met someone who was travelling with an old time friend on voyage with a lot of sea days. As the first days evolved it became evident that the situation was not going to work out because of misunderstandings between them. The person ended up joining with other travellers instead and over the next week or so and had a great time meeting other people. During that time, the roommate made a concerted effort to make this person's life miserable by their words and actions. This person rose above the situation and with dignity, and did a great job not to let the roommate spoil their cruise.

I had another experience where I met a lady who was a solo cruiser. She had made plans to cruise with another solo traveller she had met on a previous cruise. They had stayed in contact over the years and planned to do the same cruise and share expenses. It turned out that they were incompatible on several levels such as sleep patterns, activity choices, flexibility and the ability to communicate their differences. I encouraged her to articulate her specific needs, to listen to the other person's side of the situation and in a nonjudgmental way decide on a compromise that they would both be happy with. They decided that they would not dine together, although they would both participate in one of the trivia's together each day. Through clear and respectful communication, they were able to have an enjoyable cruise experience.

To be a good travel buddy, you need an open mind and the ability to negotiate along the way. This is a rule for life in general, as well as while you are travelling. Being open to new experiences and realising that your individual perspective is not always the only way, will make you a very good travel buddy. Life is full of compromises and travel is no different, it will test you every day. Part of the solution to issues that arise when you travel, is how you respond to the issue in the first instance.

Finding your own space to take a break from your cruise buddy may not always be possible. In our modern, crazy world, we may not have the opportunity to just pick up and leave, so taking some alone time can be beneficial to regroup yourself. Putting on your headphones and zoning out for a few hours can work wonders. Listening to your own music on an iPad or phone can re-centre you, so that you can move on with the adventures ahead.

Being willing to compromise is an important trait of a good cruise buddy. While it might be nice being right all the time, sometimes it's more important to just let it go. By compromising on some situations, you may have a great experience that you may not have considered before. Be an adult, don't hold a grudge, just take a deep breath and let whatever the issue is go. Life's too short.

Now this next suggestion is not going to be greeted with excitement by everyone, but believe me, you need to move with the times. A good travel buddy carries an unlocked smartphone, with a local SIM card with data, or a roaming plan with your telecommunications provider. It is becoming the modern day *must have* travel item. Let me tell you, having an active phone while travelling can ease tension. You can use the maps so you don't get lost while exploring a new town, the currency converter, the torch or compass feature, the camera, or a first aid guide. The list is endless. My advice is that at least one of your travelling party invest in taking a smartphone. It will make you an instant good travel buddy. I have devoted a blog post to this exact subject. Have a read:

bit.ly/JCCWhat2DoWithYourSmartphone

Some days personalities just don't gel. You may be travelling with a work friend who you get on well with at work, but in the real world, some things do not translate as smoothly. You'll probably find that you may require some personal space at times, so it is important to just say so.

Now this strategy may sound very harsh, but sometimes hard decisions have to be made. While it is not always possible, have a serious discussion with your travel buddy about having to part ways. Just listen to the rationale before you yell at me. *It is not a bad thing to travel alone.* Travelling alone is a great personal learning experience. Within a safe environment, take an opportunity to part ways from your travel buddy and re-join them or regroup in a few days. Consider it like an adult's time out. You never know what new interesting people and adventures you may have. All you have to do is communicate about a location or neutral zone to reconnect.

I was always lucky, as my cruise buddy for a long time was my son. We cruised over the years and it was interesting to see how his independence developed. In the earlier years when he was around 9 or 10 years old, and depending on the cruise line, he liked a combination of spending time in the kids' club, and spending time with me. As he got older, he preferred more of the kid's club activities than spending any time with me. I used to see that the major family time we spent was during shore excursions and him asking for money. He would often say, 'When you see me in the group, just walk on past.' So on the very last cruise we did together (which was a cruise to New Zealand for his Grade 12 graduation gift), I saw him with his group of cruise friends I so walked right past him, pretending to ignore him and his group of friends. He came up to me afterward and said, 'I was over there with the group, did you see me?' Sorry, mate I must have missed that. One rule of being a parent, is that you will never win.

The one cardinal rule I had while cruising with my son was we had to meet up for the evening meal. It is one way to catch up on the day's events and plan the next day's activities. He would barely have put the last spoon of dessert in his mouth before he would rush off to re-join the kids club or group activities. Travel is the best thing for children. The exposure to new experiences can make them more confident in new situations, flexible, resourceful and comfortable with change.

Finding someone to travel or cruise with can sometimes be a challenge. If you do not have a partner, family member or a friend to travel with, look for an alternative. If you cannot find someone to travel with there are a variety of websites and travel groups that cater to solo travellers, or single women. There may be a travel club in your community, or members of your local service group such as Lions or Rotary. Ladies, Red Hats Group may be worth investigating. The potential is endless. It is important to remember, however, that the person you could potentially travel with will want to do their own thing and may have their own agenda, different to yours.

If you want to have a cruise experience that is guided by you, focused on you, and have the best cruise experience possible, then potentially hiring a professional cruise companion could be the solution for you. With a professional cruise companion, you decide on the agenda, as the end goal is for you to have your amazing cruise experience. By hiring a professional cruise companion, you have the reassurance that they have the skills, knowledge and experience that is going to make your cruise experience smoother.

The more I travel, the more I find that if you travel with an open heart, an open mind, respect and understanding, things generally go pretty well. This is also why before a cruise assignment with a professional cruise companion, it is important to set boundaries, devise code words or phrases, and strategies to resolve any potential issues. A major part of a successful cruise companion relationship is communication. During the preparation phase, everyone involved has conversations around developing strategies to deal with different situations. Some strategies may be agreed phrases to defuse situations, or mutually agreed upon actions to take to keep everyone safe. For example, an agreed phrase may be required if one person needs to rest. You may not want to slow down and rest, so the cruise companion might use an ice-breaker phrase, such as, 'It is about time for a sit down (or lie) down to regather our energy'.

There will always be inconveniences and things may go wrong when you travel, so communication is important. A good cruise or trip starts with planning and preparing ahead of time. This is where as a professional cruise companion, I organise your cruise and travel to run smoothly by taking proactive steps to work through the itinerary that you plan. When you are in the booking stage, I as the cruise companion will walk you through each day of the itinerary, describing the timings and activities required to meet that day's agenda. For example, on a planned transit day we will discuss what to expect with commuting times, transport options and hotel reservations.

As a professional cruise companion, part of my role is to actively make cautious plans which will be key to stress free cruising. This could include formulating potential backup plans that allow extra time to get to cruise terminal or airport, or troubleshooting a broken piece of equipment. I may also encourage you to attend an event you might not have considered interesting. By talking over alternative plans and strategies before leaving home and formulating our 'Plan B', you will find that if these alternative plans are needed and then put into action, your trip is not adversely disrupted. With an open mind, your world will continue to open. Sharing the experience with others can be part of the fun.

So in summary, when you travel it is important to be:

- ☑ Well prepared about the destination,
- ☑ Flexible,
- ☑ A good listener,
- ☑ Open communicator,
- ☑ Drama-free,
- ☑ Easy going,
- ☑ Open minded,
- ☑ Kind,
- ☑ Patient,
- ☑ Positive,

- ☑ Sharing,
- ☑ Generous,
- ☑ Considerate,
- ☑ Compromising,
- ☑ Prepared to share,
- ☑ Adaptable,
- ☑ Accommodating,
- ☑ Contribute where you can,
- ☑ Deal with any issues,
- ☑ Become a partnership,
- ☑ Control your reactions,
- ☑ Aware of varying stress levels,
- ☑ Able to handle awkward moments,
- ☑ Accepting of other people's opinions.

When you travel, *do not* be:

- ☑ High-maintenance,
- ☑ Dramatic,
- ☑ An over packer,
- ☑ Argumentative,
- ☑ Blamer,
- ☑ Spoilsport.

If you are getting angry while travelling, ask yourself, are you,

A. Tired,
B. Hungry,
C. Thirsty,
D. All of the above.

When you are travelling either by yourself or with other people it helps to practice patience and mindfulness. Some useful strategies we like to use are from meditation practices, such as taking a few deep breaths and acknowledging what you are feeling at that moment. There will be a magic in every exact stressful moment, that you will laugh about one day, regardless of how you feel about it right now. Today's experience will become the campfire or Christmas Day story of the future. As the old adage says, it is not about the destination, it is about the journey.

Keep an Open heart, and an Open mind.

Be a good cruise buddy, good karma will come back to you sooner or later.

All Hands on Deck:
- Ask family and friends to see who might want to go with you on a cruise
- Contact Jules Cruise Companion for more information: julie@julescruisecompanion.com.au or visit the website at: www.julescruisecompanion.com.au
- Speak to your travel buddy and see what they want to do.

9

Iceberg!

'A ship in port is safe, but that's not what ships are built for.'
~ Grace Hopper

Just like on land, accidents happen and things won't always go according to plan. If you are the type of person to throw your hands into the air and gives up at any obstacle, you are probably not a person I would want on a ship anyway. Every problem has a solution, and in this chapter we will look at ways to address some common cruise related issues. This includes coping with seasickness, avoiding common illness while on board, what happens when someone passes away on board, why travel insurance is important and some general security measures. All the advice given in this chapter is general in nature, and should be taken as a guide only.

Sea Sickness

One comment I receive a lot is, '*I get sea sick*'. For those who suffer from genuine motion sickness then maybe a cruise is not for you. However, if you have been sick once on a small boat, ferry or sailboat, ocean cruising is a completely different sensation. I don't suffer from motion sickness, except if I am on a tender, and I choose to not let those 20 minutes of sensation rule my life. I have experienced rough weather all over the world, from the Atlantic Ocean to coming through Sydney Heads. As with every sensation, the motion sickness passes. I simply choose not to fixate on it.

There are precautionary strategies that you can take, such as Dramamine patches, pressure point wristbands, reducing the amount of alcohol consumed, eating a green apple or eating ginger, keeping your eyes on the horizon, or getting a balcony stateroom so that you can see the horizon. It is well known that mid ship on a low deck is the most stable place, where you feel less motion of the ocean. When rough weather is predicted, sick bags appear all around the ship. For a fee the medical staff at the sick bay can give you an injection or tablet is sometimes free at the pursers' desk.

Stability and Seasickness

Current cruise ship designs appear top heavy, as they are high with more staterooms with balconies. The logic would say this makes ships susceptible to side wind and waves, where in reality the ships are very stable. The lightweight construction of the upper decks are counterweighted by the heaviest components such as the engines, propellers, fuel tanks etc. located in the lower parts of the ship.

The width of modern cruise ships also considerably increases ship stability, with its wider centre of gravity and the ship's buoyancy. Most passenger ships have large fins or stabilisers that can be deployed to reduce rolling in heavy weather. Stabilises do not contribute to overall stability of the ship, as they are usually only employed for passenger comfort. The upshot of this is get a stateroom on lower deck and in the middle of the ship to avoid motion sickness.

Cruise/Travel Insurance

Accidents can happen, and it is important to carry cruise/travel insurance so you are not caught out. I have had a couple of incidents where it was beneficial to have this insurance. When I was in Copenhagen, I fell on a cobble path. I was on a shore excursion, so at the first opportunity I had, I notified the tour escort. When I got back to the ship, my wrist and ankle were still sore so I went the medical centre on-board and completed the standard medical forms as well as the incident form for the cruise line.

After my initial assessment with x-rays, it turned out I had chipped a bone in my wrist and had a soft tissue injury on my ankle. The treatment plan was for me to wear a wrist brace for 10 days and an ankle support for a week. After my assessment and treatment which also included an injection, I signed the forms and the cost was billed to my on-board account. The challenge with wearing a wrist brace was that I could not use a knife and fork to cut solid food, so for a few weeks I had to make a conscious effort to order food that could be eaten with a spoon.

It is important to know that if you are going to make an insurance claim, you need to have an itemised medical statement from the treating medical officer, a copy of your on board account with evidence that the account has been paid, and a copy of a bank statement verifying this payment.

When I returned home, I went through the process to make an insurance claim. This involved producing the documentary evidence of the claim mention above, and obtaining an additional medical form to be completed by my own General Practitioner.

I also had an incident in Oman, where I broke a tooth after eating a date from a market vendor, that had a stone in it. I made an inquiry to the insurance company about the potential process to follow if I was going to make a claim for treatment of this broken tooth. They sent me the specific information I needed, and it stated that a tooth could not have had any previous treatment. As my damaged tooth had a filling, it did not qualify to make a claim. I had the tooth treated with the application of a crown, which I paid for myself with no insurance claim.

Common Illness
This next section is not going to address every potential illness you may encounter on board, but will provide a general overview of measures you can adopt to avoid potential issues.

Norovirus
Norovirus is the most common cause of gastroenteritis. With a 24 hour incubation period, the symptoms of Norovirus usually last between 1 and 3 days and generally will resolve without treatment or long term consequences. In reality the likelihood of catching this illness is very low, less than 1% of more than 100 million cruise passengers and crew.

Outbreaks of norovirus are primarily transmitted person-to-person among passengers. Ship board water supplies are not responsible for the spread of the virus. The spread comes from living in close quarters, and the constant flow of new passengers who inadvertently bring viruses onto the cruise ship. Cruise ships all over the world are governed by regulations and sanitation programs, with formal plans in place to address disease outbreaks and prevention.

There are norovirus outbreaks in nursing homes, schools, day cares or hospitals all the time, without regulations of mandatory notification. The only reason norovirus outbreaks on cruise ships appears prevalent is because the regulations, tracking and notification process, are more rigorous on sea than on land.

Enterotoxigenic Escherichia Coli (ETEC)

A form of E. coli, Enterotoxigenic Escherichia coli is the leading bacterial cause of diarrhoea, especially for travellers. Causes of E. coli infections include the consumption of contaminated food, or the ingestion of water in swimming pools contaminated by human waste. Very few cases are reported worldwide. Visit the Cruise Junkie website or the US Centre for Disease Control site for further information.

Legionnaires' Disease

There are different pathogens which can colonise in pools and spas. The one you hear about on cruise ships is the bacteria, Legionella, which causes Legionnaires' disease. A virulent strain of Legionella, Legionella pneumophila serogroup 1, can cause infections when inhaled as an aerosol.

If a person has a pre-existing chronic cardiac or respiratory disease, or compromised immunity they are more susceptible to the Legionella bacteria. The cruise industry has a strict sanitation program with specific public health requirements to control and prevent Legionella.

Influenza or Common Cold or Cruise Cough

Influenza is the most frequently identified virus related illness on ships. The hacking sound is uncomfortable for the patient and those around them, so the goal is to limit potential contact and minimise the spread.

Practical proactive strategies include:

- ☑ Visiting the travel medical doctor before you leave home, to collect a medicine pack to address potential illnesses,
- ☑ At first signs of a virus:
  - ✓ Keep up fluids,
  - ✓ Take simple analgesia to treat symptoms such as fever,
  - ✓ Limit alcohol intake,
  - ✓ Increase natural fruit juices,
  - ✓ Consider taking supplemental vitamins.

Strategies to limit the spread of the virus:

- ☑ Cough into the crook of your arm,
- ☑ Wash your hands in warm soapy water and dry well,
- ☑ Use hand sanitiser,
- ☑ Use disposable tissues,
- ☑ Don't share drinking cups or utensils,
- ☑ Use paper towel to open bathroom doors,
- ☑ Use your elbow or back of your hand to activate accessible door openers or elevator buttons.

If the condition worsens, take doctor prescribed medication

- ☑ Breathing medication such as asthma medication,
- ☑ Antibiotics.

Medical Emergency Evacuation

If a passenger requires immediate medical assistance that cannot be provided by the medical facility on board, they may require removal from the ship. This situation may require a medical evacuation to the nearest medical facility. The captain and the medical officer will work with local authorities, port authorities and coast guards to facilitate the needs of the patient are met, and the itinerary of the ship may be altered in these circumstances. This may seem like an inconvenience for the thousands of other passengers, as they may miss a port or have their plans changed. However in reality, your humanity and compassion for the person in need will outweigh your disappointment about the changed plans. I have experienced these situations over the years and it shatters me to hear some of the sentiments and feelings expressed by other passengers. I take time to remind people that it is easy to be negative and it takes effort to be charitable and positive. Sometimes, the greatest gift is to look outside yourself and accept that you are not in control.

Security Screening

There are standard rules since 9/11 that all passengers have to abide by. Regardless of whether you think they are reasonable or warranted, they are the rules. International ship and flight regulations are similar and most government regulations restrict the amount of liquids, aerosols and gels you can take on board. This means that containers must be no bigger than 100ml each and be sealed in a transparent zip-lock bag (no more than 1L). Each passenger is allowed one zip-lock bag.

Other prohibited items include some sporting goods, tools and kitchen utensils with sharp edges capable of causing injury. Different rules apply for domestic and international flights, so keep yourself aware of the regulations and any changes, as rules change all the time. Refer to the cruise lines and airline's website for up to date information.

For all forms of travel:

- ☑ If you have to carry hypodermic needles, present documentation and identification at check-in,
- ☑ Never leave your baggage unattended,
- ☑ Always do your own packing,
- ☑ Use a TSA preferred lock,
- ☑ You may cling wrap your luggage at the airport for a fee,

- ☑ Pack your valuables into your carry-on luggage,
- ☑ To easily identify your luggage make it stand out,
- ☑ Have a bag of essentials with you at all times, including:
  - ✓ Medications,
  - ✓ Travel itinerary,
  - ✓ Change of clothes,
  - ✓ Water and snacks,
  - ✓ List of emergency contacts,
  - ✓ Photocopies or electronic copies of important legal documents.

Safety & Security

Security is very strong on cruise ships. A recent focus on the party culture aboard cruise ships has prompted stricter security measures. This includes the introduction of security sniffer dogs, an increased and visible security presence, closed-circuit surveillance cameras, and responsible drinking regulations.

Close Circuit Cameras are everywhere for the protection of passengers and crew. I have only had a couple of encounters with security in all my cruises, one was on Carnival Sensation and another on Sea Princess. On Carnival Sensation, we had a bottle of alcohol in the checked luggage to meet TSA security criteria, so it remained in the checked luggage when we arrived at the ship. The ship security detected the bottle and confiscated the luggage. When we were notified, we went to security office to collect the luggage minus the alcohol. We had the option of collecting the alcohol on the last morning of the cruise. My Sea Princess to Papua New Guinea experience was not as exciting. I purchased a drinks package, and every time I would pass a member of the security team they would all say, 'Hello Julie' or, 'Good Morning Julie'. How did they know my name?! I wondered if my name was on a security watch list. A reminder that Big Brother is watching.

Additional Ways to Stay Safe

The principle way to stay safe on your cruise is to pre-plan. If you will be staying in a hotel, it is advantageous to inform the staff ahead of time of any specific needs. If the person you are travelling with experiences memory issues, a change in environment may trigger anxiety or wandering. New environments may be difficult to navigate and increase stress levels. Another strategy to stay safe is by taking precautions, such as registering and wearing a MedicAlert® bracelet. When you are making travel arrangements with a person who experiences memory issues (such as dementia), it is beneficial to travel during the time of day that is best for the person.

Security

A cruise has the same crime risks as a holiday on land. There is the potential for crime everywhere. Just remain vigilant and don't put yourself in a situation that will attract the wrong kind of attention. Crimes on board and at ports vary, from theft, piracy, right up to murder. So be vigilant and don't take risks. Ship security is similar to airport security, with metal detectors, body scanning, weapon and drug detection, and vigilant photo identification scanning when getting on and off the ship.

Theft

It is not uncommon for most cruise passengers to be affluent, carry considerable amount of cash and jewellery, or even have substantial ransom potential in some developing nations. Each stateroom has a safe to keep valuables in. Most crew are trustworthy, so taking reasonable steps, such as not leaving valuables in view will keep your things safe. However there is always the potential of being robbed or scammed at a port. I always choose to keep my money and credit cards in two different places. If one goes missing, it is disappointing, but not catastrophic as I still have an alternative, on my person, usually in my bra.

For a few extra ideas about money safety check out one of my YouTube videos:

bit.ly/JCCKeepMoneySafe

Death at Sea

Sadly, this happens more often than one might think. Some say deaths on cruises could be as high as 3 people per week worldwide. So what happens when a passenger passes away while at sea or in a foreign port? What happens to the person's body? What do family or friends have to do?

Cruise lines have procedures for dealing with these unfortunate situations. This can include crew specifically trained to provide emotional and logistical support to grieving loved ones and friends. Though not grief counsellors, crew are trained to help deal with the details such as repatriating a body, contacting funeral homes, assisting friends and families work with local authorities, making travel arrangements and dealing with insurance companies. Most cruise lines will allow free Internet and phone on board and some may also do post-cruise follow-up.

Every oceangoing cruise vessel is required to carry body bags and maintain a morgue. Don't be concerned, this facility is separate from any food storage areas; most morgues are small, with room for up to three to six bodies. There is no hard and fast rule about what happens to the body as different considerations influence whether the body has to be immediately repatriated from a foreign port, or could stay on-board depending on location of the ship at the time of its itinerary. Some smaller nations may not have the equipment and infrastructure to deal with the repatriation of a body or have laws about the movement of human remains.

When the body is offloaded, it will be done so into the care of a medical examiner's office and arrangements made with local rules and regulations for repatriation. There may be consular support available to help in making arrangements with local authorities. Consular services can even serve as provisional conservator of the person's estate if no one else is able to do it. Cost for services, support and repatriation are paid by the family, friends or estate. It is important to also notify the person's insurer as most cruise/travel insurance plans, do cover the bulk of these expenses.

Pirates

While most cruise lines have generally avoided arming security guards or crew for reasons of liability, safety, and conformity with the local laws of the countries visited, you will find that cruise ships have small arms (usually semi-automatic pistols) stored in a safe accessible only by the captain who distributes them to authorised personnel such as master-at-arms or security. All cruise lines have a pirate protocol that will include turning off all lights, and passengers being ordered immediately below deck. The stabilisers will be stowed to make the ship's wake more severe, and the ship will commence manoeuvres, alternately sweeping the vessel in exaggerated movements port and starboard as in the incident with *MSC Melody* in April 2009. An initial aim would be to outrun any potential threat, a ship could often be maneuvered to ram a pirate craft. In the case of potential pirate attack, ships are also equipped with high-pressure fire hoses that can be used to repel boarders. A recent technology to deter pirates has been the Long Range Acoustic Device or sonic cannon which was used in the successful defence of 115 passengers on *Seabourn Spirit* on 5 November 2005 when she was attacked by two pirate speed boats off Somalia.

When travelling through known troubled waters such as the Indian Ocean, the Arabian Sea or the Gulf of Aden, different cruise lines implement different strategies to address security concerns for pirates. Recently transiting the Suez Canal, the captain ordered a practice pirate drill, where passengers move into the public spaces in the centre of the ship. In addition to the drill we also had a 5 night blackout plan for the ship. An additional layer of security was employed during the passage through the Suez Canal as the cruise line hired a third party security firm. Ex-British Special Forces working for an International Security Firm boarded and stayed on board until we had passed the water of Yemen, Djibouti and Somalia.

Muster/Lifeboat Drill

In order to comply with the International Convention for the Safety of Life at Sea, all passenger ships must have a cruise mandatory muster drill during the first 24 hours of the cruise. Refer to Chapter 5, All Aboard, for more information.

All Hands on Deck:
- Investigate insurance policies that might suit your specific needs
- Check out my bonus information on my blog on how to avoid missing your cruise ship, and what to do if you do: bit.ly/JCCHow2AvoidMissingYourCruiseShip
- Read my blog for information on my standard medical kit: bit.ly/JCCRevisedMedPack

10

Little Ship Mates

'The difference between a fairy tale and a sea tale? A fairy tale starts with "Once upon a time". A sea tale starts with "This ain't no $hit".'

~ Edith Widder

When travelling with children you are completely responsible for them. There is no break, you need to have a plan for them the whole trip, 24/7. They need to be fed regularly, sheltered, kept safe, entertained and educated etc. When planning a trip with a child you need to balance your needs and their needs. It is unrealistic to believe that you are going to have a holiday that just suits you and everyone else has to ride along obediently. It is important for children to have a say in the activities. During my planning phase I would sit down with my son and have a conversation about what attractions or activities he wanted to see and do. It is also important that the child knows that it is ok not to like everything that is being planned and people have different interests.

If the child is not travelling with their parent or legal guardian, for example travelling with a family friend on holidays, additional papers and authorities have to be signed and carried with you throughout your whole journey. Advice in this chapter is general in nature. If there are legal or custodial issues with your child, seek the appropriate legal advice.

Planning
At this time I would start having conversations with my son regarding my expectations of behaviour during the trip. You have to prepare the child for the experience they are about to have. This means explaining that there may be times when they are bored, hungry, tired, disinterested, frustrated, overwhelmed or even scared. All of these feelings and emotions are very normal and they are all OK. I would teach my son strategies to build resilience, tolerance and ability to compromise. I would expect him to acknowledge the emotions and feelings and move on.

What is important is that a child needs to have the experiences and evaluate them in perspective. It was important that he knew that it was not OK to quit when confronted with new and overwhelming experiences. When you were confronted with a new challenging issue, you take a step back, evaluate it and devise a new plan or strategy.

Boredom is a natural part of life and can be a big issue to address when travelling with children. There is no law to say a child has to be entertained and distracted all day, every day. However there seems to be a fixation on instant gratification and continual bombardment with input such as social media or electronic devices. Being bored builds tolerance, patience and imagination. If a child is given reasonable guidance about the feelings around being bored, they can manage themselves when the time comes. My son learned really quickly not to complain.

Passports and Visas
Check with your travel agent or the embassy of the nation you are visiting if your child needs a passport and visa. Child passports are usually valid for a shorter time than adult passports, so be vigilant that your child's passport meets the criteria for travel. Normally it is required that passports be valid 6 months after the date of travel. Always allow yourself enough time to renew passports when planning your trip.

Visiting Sites of Significance
Travelling with children is not about self, we are citizens of the world. It is about taking opportunities to learn where you fit into the world around you. I see an obligation for parents to teach children about how and why they are living in the often privileged circumstances that they are. By this, I mean teaching children about the sacrifices of past generations that allow us the freedom and privilege we enjoy today. One of the primary things I did when I travelled with my son, was on every trip we would visit at least one war memorial, war cemetery or holocaust museum. It is also very important for children to learn a variety of perspectives of major historical events. Attend memorials from other cultures, to gain a perspective that may be different from your personal beliefs. I acknowledge this can

be an emotional experience, and unpleasant at times. However, as part of personal growth, I feel it is a valuable experience that should be embraced.

In addition, visiting places of worship from different denominations and religions provides exposure to different philosophies than your own. There is the potential to develop tolerance, understanding and mutual respect.

Safety
When you are travelling with children you cannot relax your supervision level. Holidays and travel have additional dangers you have to be aware of. It is important that children feel safe so that they are not in a constant state of fear, that they have enjoyable interactions with local people without the fear of being abducted. It may be worth investating a child locator or GPS tracker. They are a small transmitter that you place on your child on their clothing which allows you to follow your child's position on an app, if you are to get separated. It is worth tagging your child with a label with your name and phone number so if the child is lost, someone has a way of contacting you. I have known some parents to write their phone number on their child's arm, though this has not been a strategy that I ever employed. Dressing your child in bright clothing may assist in easy recognition in busy areas.

An advantage of a cruise holiday is that the cost of Kids Club activities are included in the price of the cruise. You have a level of reassurance that the service offered meets specific guidelines and criteria, with suitably trained staff. For younger children up to about 3 years of age, there may be services offered for an additional fee. For children up to 16 years, most cruise lines have age appropriate activities each day. With the younger age groups, parents or guardians sign the children in and out of the Kids Club, while for older children the process is more relaxed. Most cruise lines will have a service where the children are supervised during meal times if not with parents. Kids Club times and activities will have published in the daily cruise newsletter.

General Health and Safety

Becoming unwell on your holiday is not going to be fun for anyone. Prepare to stay healthy by checking any immunisation requirements before leaving home. Take reasonable precautions against viruses and bacteria as I mentioned in the previous chapter.

A couple of additional tips are:

- ☑ If unsure about hygiene standards, it would not hurt to occasionally wipe over cutlery in restaurants with a wipe or sanitiser,
- ☑ Avoid the risks of animal bites (such as cats, dogs monkeys, etc.) by not patting local or stray animals,
- ☑ Wearing hats, sunscreen and insect repellent.

Food

There are restrictions when travelling with containers carrying liquids. Airport security can open all containers during screening, so be aware of potential contamination. Travelling may disrupt your regular meal times, so where possible try to keep to a routine for eating. You may need to rely on snack food alternatives if no meal options are available, but try to keep snacks as healthy as possible. Most restaurants will have a children's' menu, and if not, share your meal with them. There are always universal chain restaurants to get you through, and I have found that most countries have a toasted sandwich alternative such as pizza, lahmacun or pide.

If your child is of an age where bottle sterilisation is a priority, there are travel options available. If children are older and absolute sterilisation is not required, washing utensils in hot water or microwaving them may help. You have to feel comfortable with the options available to you.

In most developed nations, drinking tap water is a reasonable choice. In developing nations, it may be advisable to drink bottled or treated water. Avoid the consumption of beverages with ice made from local water.

Water Safety

Children should be taught how to swim from the earliest age possible. They must be supervised at all times around water, and not all pools or spas are enclosed, so be vigilant. Swimming pool facilities don't always have a trained lifeguard on duty, so as a parent or guardian it is your responsibility to supervise your children.

Just because you are on holidays, you cannot relax. You are ultimately responsible for your child and it is no one else's responsibility to care for and protect your child. This might sound harsh, but you can never stop being a responsible adult, even when on holidays. This is not to say that you won't have a relaxing and enjoyable holiday. Cruising can be a wonderful holiday when travelling with children.

Adult Supervision

I had a few specific rules as a parent when travelling with my child. One included the responsible consumption of alcohol. Just because you are on holidays it does not void you from parental responsibilities.

At some point you may be required to be an adult, make decisions and be there for you child. Choosing to be drunk does not relieve you of these responsibilities. This is another reason why cruising is a really great holiday option as there are often other reasonable adults (trained crew) around to help out in an emergency situation.

Down Days

When planning your trip with children it is important to factor in down days every 3rd or 4th day. These rest days could be spent by the pool or when you do the laundry. When travelling with children you don't have to be on the go every single day. It is tiring for you, and it is tiring for the child. A tired child is not going to enjoy them self and is going to make your time miserable. By proactively managing the activity levels you can often sustain a longer itinerary.

Accommodation

I always book accommodation for when I arrive in a new location, especially when travelling with my son. When you are travelling alone or with adults you can wing it when you arrive in a new location. When travelling with children you need an element of predictability and reliability for your trip to run smoothly. When booking accommodation, I always choose to stay in central location in the area. I use it as my base and explore a different area each day. When booking hotels I check reviews using websites such as TripAdvisor. I use online booking portals, and filter the search until I get my desired location, price and amenities to align. I also go onto google maps and check out the location, assessing for proximity to noisy highways or steep hills or streets. By using the street view function I am able to see the surrounding streets and identify local amenities such as convenience stores, public transport and restaurants.

Depending on the age of your child, consider accommodation on lower levels of buildings to avoid balconies. You may also want to consider a holiday rental such as Airbnb. It was never something I did, though it does give you more options when considering meal patterns and budgeting. Some hostels have family rooms which provides an added flexibility when travelling with children.

Transportation

If travelling with children by plane, give yourself additional time for check in and transfers, factoring in sleep patterns and time to eat. When booking your flight, make sure you order kids meals or any additional dietary requirements. For long haul flights, is it is often better travelling at night, when the child would be in a natural sleeping pattern.

If you have an airport connection, allow extra time especially if you are unfamiliar with the airport or it is a large or busy terminal. On a layover you may be able to take advantage of a children's play area where they can let off steam and tire themselves out before the next leg of the flight. Online check-in may help to reduce stress so when you arrive at the airport all you have to do is go to the baggage drop off. There is no escaping the security processes, so allow yourself additional time for that.

Most airlines offer assistance or early boarding for travellers with smaller children. Regulations vary between airlines as to when a child must have their own seat on a plane.

An uncomfortable time for a child may be take-off and landing where the change in cabin pressure may hurt the child's ears. Some tips to help include giving the child something to eat and drink, or chewing gum for older children. There may be over the counter ear drops you could purchase before you leave on your trip. Don't forget to take things to occupy the child such as an electronic tablet or small games. It is also important to have a conversation with your child to talk about the experience and explain your expectations of their behaviour and introduce the concept of being respectful of other passengers.

Be proactive and choose a seat on the plane that best suits your family's needs. For example, sitting near the back may be more convenient to access the bathroom or have areas to stand up, however it may have a trade-off with being a bit nosier. Bulkhead seats in the middle of plane may offer more legroom and a small area for a child to sit on the floor to play. For a younger child, arrange for a bassinet. The window or the aisle debate is one that will be a personal preference. Explore which option may work best for you.

Travelling with children on trains can often be enjoyable as there is more facility to walk and move around compared to a plane, bus or car.

Travelling in cars or taxis when on holidays is a very common mode of transport. When hiring a car, depending on the age of the children, you may need to consider taking child's car seat or hiring one when you get to your destination. This may not always be possible in taxis or Ubers. Make a reasonable effort when booking services to have safety needs met. Seat belt laws are in place in most developed nations, while in developing nations these laws may not be enforced. It is up to you to make reasonable decisions about child safety in each individual circumstance.

Orientation

When I first visit a new area, I take time to orientate myself. I usually use a Hop-On Hop-Off or trolley service, and with set routes linking major tourist attractions, it can be a cost effective way to get around. Once in Las Vegas we stayed off the Strip, and the trolley service went to the Atomic Museum which was very close to our hotel. It was convenient in this case to use the Hop-On Hop-Off bus as our standard way to get around. If the city you are visiting has a Metro or Subway system, study the map before you leave home. It can also be a fantastic way to orientate and get around a city quickly.

Another strategy I find useful is to take a free walking tour. In New York I used Apple Greeters, a free service where interested locals show you their unique part of the city. My Apple Greeter was a physiotherapist from Belvedere Hospital. She came to the hotel to collect us, took us to the underground and offered to show us how to purchase a travel pass. She took us to Brooklyn and DUMBO (Down Under the Manhattan Bridge Overpass), an area I would never have visited by myself.

When I returned to New York on another trip, I did a huge walk to over the bridge again, because of that wonderful experience the first time. The next time I went to New York it was Labor Day and I had gained the confidence of being in unfamiliar areas. I made contact with trade union comrades and participated in the Labor Day Parade in Queens, first walking for about 2.5km and then riding on a float. The amazing nurses danced with an infectious energy and I even had my photo taken with New York Police officers.

There were so many advantages to travelling with my son. On a few occasions when my stress levels were high, he had a great ability to break the ice and make me laugh. He became good at managing money through budgeting and planning, and he also became good at time keeping. We have lots of photo books of our adventures together, and my gift to the world was a well-travelled child.

All Hands on Deck:
- Check out the kid's club criteria on any of the cruise line's websites
- Check out Disney Cruise Lines
- Start a conversation with your child, put the information on the planner spreadsheet
- Check out the packing list for children in the resource section of this book.

11

Ahoy, Me Hearty

'Twenty years from now you will be more disappointed by things you didn't do than by the ones you did do. So throw off the bowlines, sail away from the safe harbour. Catch the winds in your sails. Explore. Dream. Discover.'

~ Mark Twain

What is the appeal of cruising if you have a disability? A cruise holiday is suitable for anybody, even if a member of your party has special needs, such as mobility impairment, dementia, Alzheimer's, or Parkinson's Disease. Most cruise lines work to accommodate special needs so that everyone in the family has an enjoyable holiday. If you cruise from a port close to home, the whole experience can become even easier. As a savvy cruiser you can become knowledgeable, educating yourself on policies that can help you enjoy your dream cruise.

What Does 'Accessible' Mean?

Accessibility is a universal description for a group of inconsistent physical access standards. As you travel, you may find that public access to some facilities are described as accessible, when in reality they are not. Some facilities may have a ramp with a steep gradient, or may have two or three steps that is described as disability accessible. There will be a lot of frustrations if you don't do your research and travel to wrong destinations.

Understanding Your Specific Needs

Travelling of any kind, with any form of disability, takes some additional planning. When booking travel you need to explain your needs to the travel company, cruise line or airline staff. It has to be understood that while cabin and ground staff at the airport or cruise terminal may have no specialist medical training, they are ready to assist you wherever possible.

Consider the following questions, will you:

- ☑ Be able to get to the cruise terminal, or airport?
- ☑ Be travelling with a carer, assistant or alone?
- ☑ Need help checking in and handling the luggage?
- ☑ Need assistance getting around the cruise terminal or airport?

- ☑ Require help boarding?
- ☑ Require an elevator?
- ☑ Be able to find and access the toilet on the ship or plane?
- ☑ Be able to understand safety briefings and instructions from staff? (Are sign interpreters, braille or large-print books available?).
- ☑ Prepared if you should have an accident?
- ☑ Be able to fit a scooter through the stateroom doorway?

Exploring the world should be an enjoyable and relaxing experience for everyone. Unfortunately, with a disability there may be challenges that could potentially make travel unpleasant. Even though most countries have legislations to deal with accessibility issues to make it easier for disabled people to travel, you still may encounter obstacles, challenges, misunderstandings and confusion. Regardless of the disability, with planning and communication you can still have a safe and enjoyable holiday.

When travelling with someone with special needs, there are a few things you can do to try to make the travel experience smoother. It is important to be patient as not all employees know the legal rights for people with disabilities or are willing to give assistance. Keep communicating calmly and consistently in all situations and keep seeking workable solutions.

Cruise Lines and Air Travel

All cruise lines, airlines and airports are governed by a Disability Discrimination legislation in their relevant country, to provide services for people with disability.

Trained staff should be available to assist with:

- ☑ Handling luggage,
- ☑ Getting around the terminal,
- ☑ Getting on and off the ship or plane,

- ☑ Getting to and from the plane toilet (in the case of a semi-ambulant person),
- ☑ Meals, such as opening packaged meals,
- ☑ Delivering safety briefings in a way that all passengers can understand.

It has to be understood that ship's crew or airline or airport staff are not expected to assist with personal processes such as eating, administering medication, using the toilet or lifting or carrying a passenger.

Airport Security

When you use a mobility aid or a wheelchair, and you are unable to pass through the metal detector without it, security staff may use a handheld device to search you. Security staff might also search in and around the mobility aid. If the security option is a physical search, you the traveller have the right to ask for a private room.

Choose a Cruise Itinerary for Your Ability

If you have mobility or health issues, choose an appropriate cruise itinerary. Do not choose an itinerary that involves stairs, curbs, elevators, rough surfaces such as cobblestones, or with no accessible transport options. Select an itinerary with smooth terrain, accessible transport, and attractions close to the port.

Choose Shore Excursions for Your Ability

A shore excursion is a third party optional activity sold by the cruise line. Activities range in activity level, from passive bus rides, to active snorkelling, to zip lining, to walking ancient ruins. Excursion descriptions should disclose accessibility level and any restrictions. As a cruiser with accessibility or mobility issues, you may want to make alternative arrangements, such as through a travel agent or local tour operator before leaving home.

General Ports
On an embarkation or disembarkation, port access is consistently a reasonable standard. While ships in general are relatively accessible, ports and shore excursions may not be. With each port of call, access via gangway or ramps to the ship change. At times, the gangway may be very steep. It may have small bars across the walkway, or some gangways may be small steps. When able, there will be dedicated crew at the exit point to assist wheelchair and mobility passengers.

Tenders
When the ship visits a port that lacks dock availability or inclement weather it may mean that the ship may anchor offshore. The cruise line will shuttle passengers to the port in small boats called tenders. To avoid disappointment, take some time before you book your cruise to assess your chosen itinerary, and investigate your cruise line's policy on mobility aid access to tenders. You will find that passengers who have trouble walking or use mobility devices may not be allowed on the tender for a port visit or shore excursion. As some ports only use a tender, it will not be a wise itinerary choice for you.

Choose the Cruise Duration
If you haven't cruised before, consider the length of time you would like to spend on a cruise. As a test, you may want to take a short cruise, which can serve a couple of purposes. Firstly, it can test how you respond within the shipboard environment, the lifts, bathroom access, public bathroom access, and negotiating the embarkation and disembarkation process. Secondly, there are often no ports of call, you just stay on the boat. If everything goes well, you might then choose to expand your experience to a longer itinerary with appropriate ports for you. Ironically, a longer cruise, such as a repositioning cruise with more sea days than port days, may be an appropriate itinerary for people with mobility or cognitive impairment issues. Another aspect to consider is the additional travel that is required to the embarkation port and from the disembarkation port.

Choose the Ship and its Facilities

With planning, support and backup plans, cruising can be a rewarding experience. Not all cruise ships are the same, even in the same fleet. Generally, newer ships are better for passengers with reduced mobility. However, as older vessels undergo refurbishments, many update their features to enhance access. For example, a ship might have automatic doors installed, or restrooms in public areas made accessible so guests don't have to return to their staterooms all the time.

Cruise ships have a limited number of accessible cabins that are specifically designed for mobility disabilities. These rooms may have wider stateroom doors, space to allow a wheelchair to turn, a roll-in shower and grab rails. Modern cruise ships may also have automated stateroom doors. Cruise lines will have accessible routes marked throughout each ship, accessible seating at dining venues and the theatre.

Most cruise lines will have a department available to answer questions about special needs. Once you have booked your cruise, passengers with disabilities will be required to complete a special needs form which will ask about the passenger's equipment and assistance that may be required from the cruise line.

At the time of booking, also notify the cruise line of any dietary requirements, such as diabetic, gluten free, halal or kosher. Many of the special services must be arranged up to 30 or 60 days prior to embarkation. Most cruise lines require passengers with disabilities to travel with a caregiver.

Swimming Pool Access

You will find that some areas such as the solarium have stairs going into the hot tub or pool, where public access pools only have ladder access. Inquire about specific access on the ship you are choosing to travel on. Some pools have a chair hoist that can be accessed with assistance of the ship's crew.

Book in Well in Advance

If you have specific needs such as accessible staterooms, adjoining staterooms or staterooms close to each other, you will need to book your cruise as far in advance as practicable. If travelling in a group with someone with special needs, consider booking adjoining staterooms as they will offer you privacy, and close access to all members of your party. It would not be unreasonable to book up to a year in advance to secure the stateroom that will best suits your needs.

Choose a Stateroom Location

When choosing a stateroom, there are few rules to consider, such as:

- ☑ Will it be easy to get to?
- ☑ Is it at the end of a hall?
- ☑ How close is it to the lifts for easy access?
- ☑ How far is it from the pool or the dining room?

A good resource is the ship's map on the company website. You can use it to assess easy routes from your stateroom to public spaces you may want to attend.

Medical Considerations

When you have decided on your cruise destination, it is time to start preparing the finer details, such as:

- ☑ Communicate your needs thoroughly and clearly to your travel agent or service providers,
- ☑ Getting medical clearance to travel or a 'Fit to Fly' letter from your medical officer,
- ☑ Medical clearance forms from the different carriers,
- ☑ Medic Alert Bracelet,
- ☑ Travel documentation.

Visit to your Medical Officer or General Practitioner for advice on:

- ☑ Travel precautions,
- ☑ Inoculations,
- ☑ Medication risks,
- ☑ Request all the medication for the length of the cruise (adding a few days extra in case of delays or you drop some),
- ☑ Documentation, a letter that includes all your conditions (including metal implants), medications and treatments, stating that you are 'Fit to Travel' or 'Fit to Fly'.

This information may help the ship's doctor in an unforeseen medical emergency.

General travel advice about documents is the same for all travellers regardless of ability, and it includes;

- ☑ Doctors' names and contact information,
- ☑ Cleared to travel or 'Fit to Fly' letter from your doctor,
- ☑ A list of current medications and dosages, keep medication in their intact packaging with visible pharmaceutical label visible,
- ☑ Carry your written prescriptions,
- ☑ Contact numbers and address of local police, fire, hospitals and poison control agencies,
- ☑ A list of food or drug allergies,
- ☑ Copies of legal papers (living will, advanced directives, power of attorney, etc.),
- ☑ Names and contact information of friends and family members to call in case of an emergency,
- ☑ Insurance information (policy number, member name),

- ☑ Carry a letter detailing your disability,
- ☑ Take deep vein thrombosis precautions,
- ☑ Carry enough medication for the journey in your carry-on luggage, not in your checked luggage,
- ☑ Keep medication that requires a low temperature in a cooler bag,
- ☑ Medical sharps from your medication should be OK, just carry a doctor's letter,
- ☑ If you need to administer medication during your journey, make sure your carer is adequately prepared.

Assistance Dogs
If you are travelling with assistance dogs, investigate each cruise company or airline as they have individual rules and regulations. When booking your flight or service, check that registered service dogs can accompany you. Some airlines allow dogs to remain on board, while others require them to be placed in a secure pet container in the hold. Some companies require you to complete a checklist about the animal's training and certification before they will accept an assistance dog on-board. Carry a laminated identification card for the animal with their name and their companion's name, ready to show to staff on request. It is important to make sure your dog has access to food, water and toilet facilities. If travelling internationally, check specifications and required documentation (vaccinations, micro-chipping, treatments etc.) for the dog to meet quarantine specifications and airport rules. A safety harness may be required for your dog during take-off, landing, or any time the 'fasten seat belt' sign is turned on.

Medical Aids
If you have a visual or hearing impairment you will find hearing assistant 'loops' and tactile (including Braille) signage at most major cruise and airport terminals. It could be helpful at security checkpoints to advise the screening officers of any medical implants (such as pacemakers or hearing aids) or prosthetic limbs, as a physical pat-down may be opted for

instead of an x-ray. There is no need to take off a hearing aid when passing through security, as they are too small to set off the metal detector, and scanners and x-rays will not damage them. Have any documentation related to your disability on hand at all times.

Getting On Board
Cruise lines make every effort to accommodate specific requests for cognitive impaired or disabled guests, though it is unrealistic to expect them to meet every request. Cruise lines offer guests with special needs priority boarding and disembarkation as well as additional assistance during these potentially stressful times.

Public Areas
Mobility around a cruise ship is pretty easy in public spaces. Most public corridors are wide, graduated passages and have wheelchair ramps, elevators and even chair lifts and stairs for some swimming pools and hot tubs. Most public bathrooms are wheelchair accessible.

Bright Colours
To make yourself easily recognisable in a crowd it may be beneficial if you consider dressing in bright colours or distinctive clothing.

Identification
Should your special need be cognitive it may be helpful to wear a wristband or a distinctive lanyard. Carry identification printed with your name, the ship name and stateroom number, along with a phone number of a contact.

Tracking Devices
Cruise ships are large. Getting lost is easy for anyone, so with cognitive challenges, it may be overwhelming. Investigate if the cruise line you have chosen has mobile devices with GPS tracking or similar for hire.

Make Your Stateroom Recognisable

When looking at corridors near your stateroom you may see them as indistinguishable from one another. What you can do is take time to decorate your stateroom door so it stands out and will be more easily recognisable. For loved ones who tend to wander, you could consider packing a travel door alarm, this will alert you when the stateroom door opens.

Plan Meals Ahead of Time

If your family member has memory issues, a cruise dining experience can be planned to meet their needs. Developing familiarity of the route to the dining room and attending the same dining table, can be comforting to a loved one. You can also investigate other dining alternatives, where the schedule is more convenient, for example dining in the buffet or room service.

Hotel Accommodation

When you are booking accommodation, most major hotel booking sites have an option to filter for accessible accommodation. By filtering for specific search criteria including facilities for people who are hearing impaired, who need braille signage, accessible parking, or a roll-in shower, for example, it offers you realistic options. It may pay to ask the hotel for a photo of the environment so that you know before you arrive if it will meet your individual needs.

There are other websites such as www.australiaforall.com and www.cangoeverywhere.com.au that have accessible accommodation directories collated by people with disability. A very good resource is the People with Disability Australia (PWDA) website. It would be worth investigating the National Information Communication Awareness Network at nican.com.au or downloading their app for support when travelling.

Bathrooms

If travelling by plane be aware that bathroom facilities are usually very small. Some planes just have a privacy curtain that can be pulled if the door is required to be left open for your assistant to support you. When booking and boarding the plane, ask the staff to make sure anything you need will be available during the flight for you to access the toilet.

Wheelchairs

If you have mobility issues and do not normally use mobility aids, you may benefit from requesting a wheelchair or wheelchair assistant at the airport or ships' terminal during transit. Most companies work on meeting special needs of guests or passengers.

If you're travelling with a wheelchair, you will find all airlines will ask you to check it in. Make enquiries with your carrier as some budget airlines won't carry electric wheelchairs at all, and those that do may disconnect the battery and carry it separately.

Some airline policies prevent the carriage of battery-operated wheelchairs as they may exceed the maximum weight limit or will charge a fee. You may consider other methods of transporting your mobility item via freight or even hire a similar product at your destination.

It is important to find out if your carrier has a *two wheelchair limit* as this policy could be seen unreasonably restrictive, unfair and discriminatory to the rights of people who need to travel with wheelchairs.

Check for Mobility and Health Equipment

Consider hiring mobility aids or medical equipment for your cruise. Due to safety regulation, all mobility equipment has to be stored in your stateroom and never in public spaces or hallways. All equipment will have guidelines such as acceptable weight or width, including the types of batteries and chargers they require. If you are bringing your own mobility equipment, have it serviced prior to travelling.

Public Transport

Major transport companies are required to make reasonable adjustments to provide accessible transport. Unfortunately, in reality many trains, taxis, buses or ferries in Australia are still not accessible. It is advisable when travelling overseas to make an effort to research the area you are wanting to travel to, as overseas transport options are more ad hoc.

Hire Cars

In most major cities, most major hire car agencies include wheelchair-accessible vehicles in their fleets. It may be beneficial to enquire with leading car hire companies, if they offer vehicles with modifications (hand controls, swivel seats and transfer boards). Investigate disability transport specialists, such as Wheelies Van Rental, Wheelaway or Disabled Motorists Australia, or similar worldwide.

Travel Insurance

Finding travel insurance may be tricky or more expensive for a person with a disability. With some effort, it is relatively easy to get travel insurance with a pre-existing condition and it's worth the additional upfront costs if something should happen while you're away. These challenges should not prevent you from buying a travel insurance policy, but you may require a letter from your medical officer about stable conditions. There are regulations that insurers must assess the actual risks, and not make assumptions about individual disabilities.

You may need to consider taking out additional insurance coverage for any mobility aids or wheelchair, hearing aid, etc. Check the Product Disclosure Statement of your chosen policy to see excluded items. You may find some travel insurance companies can cover your mobility equipment if something happens to it. Some policies could compensate replacement medication and take care of medical expenses incurred on your break. Overseas medical costs and repatriation are very expensive, so travel insurance is a must-have.

Technology

Travellers with disabilities can research so much information on line, such as passages, footpaths, accessibility ramps, and services. Technology has revolutionised the way we access and share information. It is not uncommon to zoom in on Google Earth or Google Maps to check out actual locations and how they appear in real life.

Look Into Joining a Group

First-time cruisers with disabilities might prefer travelling with a support group. Organisations such as the Dialysis at Sea, Multiple Sclerosis Foundation and the Amputee Coalition advertise cruises in newsletters and on their websites.

Consider Hiring a Professional

You can always book a cruise yourself, and be responsible for the research, the analysis of options and the outcomes. Alternatively, you can hire a service such as mine, Jules Cruise Companion. Together we can look into specialist accessible travel options that will meet your needs. We are familiar with the cruise lines and their ships, port access at destinations and together we can coordinate accessible ground transportation. A professional can make sure you book accessible hotel rooms pre- and post-cruise, as well as offer advice on renting medical equipment.

All Hands on Deck:
- Look at an accessibility website
- Some cities have access information on websites
- Check with your GP, get a travel check-up and immunisation
- Read more about cruising with special needs on my blog: bit.ly/JCCCruisingWithSpecialNeeds
- Read about getting to your cruise embarkation port by plane: bit.ly/JCCTravellingWithADisabilityViaPlane2YourCruise

12

Post Cruise Blues (PCB)

'It isn't that life ashore is distasteful to me, but life at sea is better.'
~ Sir Francis Drake

I sit here on day 19 of a 23 day Trans-Pacific cruise:

- ☑ I have written this book,
- ☑ I have laughed,
- ☑ I had a broken toilet,
- ☑ I had the best and the worst service,
- ☑ I had happy hours and drink vouchers,
- ☑ There was a medical evacuation,
- ☑ There were three people who started the cruise but didn't finish it (RIP),
- ☑ The internet was patchy,
- ☑ There was a missed port,
- ☑ There were new ports,
- ☑ There were old ports,
- ☑ I have made new lifetime friends from Germany, Canada, the USA, and Australia,
- ☑ And I had a fantastic cruise buddy.

It was a great cruise. There is no holiday experience like it. Come cruise with me!

In this chapter I will explain the feelings some people can experience when finishing a cruise, and discuss some strategies to help alleviate any sadness.

This book has laid the platform for you to book a cruise with more confidence. If you feel you require some additional assistance making that cruise booking, I will finish with some specific suggestions.

How to Beat Post-Cruise Blues (PCB)

Unfortunately no one is immune from Post-Cruise Blues (PCB). You may even call the feeling, Post-Cruise Depression (PCD) or Post-Cruise Withdrawal (PCW). For now I will just call it PCB, a Julie defined psychological state or set of feelings related to the completion of a cruise. The bonus is PCB has a defined lifespan and is treatable at all stages. It all depends on when you detect it and how aggressive you want to treat it. Sometimes disembarkation day can be a trauma, but when you get home PCB could be waiting for you. Sorry I fibbed, there is no real cure for PCB but there are some interventions you can employ to stave off the full effects.

Read Forums or Write a Review

You can start immediate PCB treatment by attempting to turn your low into a high by talking about your cruise experience. You could offer advice to others. Like me, as a cruise regular, you have knowledge that is invaluable to newbie cruisers. You might choose to write a review on cruise or travel websites such as TripAdvisor.com. Sharing your cruise hacks and tips can raise your spirits and minimise the effects of PCB.

Cruise News

There are different forums you can subscribe to, such as Cruise Critic, or Facebook pages to stay up to date with the latest cruise ship news and travel tips. You may even enjoy a weekly podcast from Cruise Radio to get your fix of cruise news. Cruise magazines or e-newsletters, could be enough to stave off a serious case of PCB. Or you could read a cruise blog (such as mine Jules Cruise Companion). The internet is good for doing cruise research but there is nothing like the joy of flicking through a hard copy, glossy, travel brochure from the travel agent.

Document Your Trip

A reasonable prescription to nurse a dose of PCB is to relive your cruise by writing about it. You can write a diary, a blog, or a travel book. Along with some photos, you can retell your adventure to share with family and friends.

Be an Unpaid Travel Consultant

Develop your expertise to help friends or family plan a cruise. When I first started cruising, very few people I knew or worked with had been on a cruise. The more I cruised, the more I talked about it, and the more people wanted to come away with me. I would leave my coffee table photo books in the tea room at work for anyone to look at. It felt thrilling when someone asked me about a trip I had been on, or where they might like to go themselves, or to let me know they had booked a cruise after being inspired by my books.

Watch Cruise Movies or Television shows

Cruise ships often appear in movies or on television shows. For example, a Fantasy-class Carnival Cruise Line ship features in 'The Birdcage', and Norwegian Spirit can be spotted in '21 Jump Street'. The following recommendations will provide you with a temporary fix.

1. *Shall We Dance?* (1937) A rom-com starring Fred Astaire and Ginger Rogers, set on a ship sailing from Paris to New York.
2. *Romance on the High Seas* (1948) is a Doris Day film with a mixed plot on a cruise to Rio.
3. *Gentlemen Prefer Blondes* (1953) starring Marilyn Monroe and Jane Russell on a cruise to Paris.
4. *An Affair to Remember* (1957) Cary Grant and Deborah Kerr, share that immortal scene at the top of the Empire State Building.
5. *Bon Voyage!* (1962) a Walt Disney movie about an ocean crossing aboard SS United States.
6. *Speed 2: Cruise Control* (1997) filmed on board *Seabourn Legend*.
7. *Parent Trap* (1998) filmed on-board Cunard's *Queen Elizabeth 2*.
8. *Boat Trip* (2002) filmed on a cruise ship out of Athens.
9. *Death on the Nile* (1978), the Whodunit filmed on location in Egypt.
10. *Pirates of the Caribbean, The Curse of the Black Pearl* (2003), The adventures or misadventures of Captain Jack Sparrow.

11. *Master and Commander: The Far Side of the World* (2003), set during the Napoleonic Wars, starring Russell Crowe as a brash British captain.
12. *Love Boat*, every episode from 1977 to 1986.

Movies you might want to give a miss:

1. *Jaws* (1975) directed by Steven Spielberg, where a giant great white shark menaces a New England beach resort, until a local sheriff teams up with a marine biologist and an old seafarer to hunt the monster down. Actor Roy Scheider, Richard Dreyfuss
2. *The Poseidon Adventure* (1972) starring Gene Hackman, Roddy McDowell, Ernest Borgnine, and Shelley Winters. This disaster movie combined disorientation of upside-down and underwater.
3. *Titanic* (1997) This is a predictable movie as you know the ending, has some special effects that make you feel like you are really on the ship. You will be singing along to the Celine Dion's theme song for days after watching this one.
4. *Captain Phillips*, is the 2013 movie depicting the true story of the first American cargo ship hijacked in two hundred years. Tom Hanks portrays Capt. Richard Phillips and the 2009 hijacking of the U.S. flagged MV Maersk Alabama by Somali pirates.

Compile a Coffee Table Photo Book

I am able to reduce some of my Post Cruise Blues by making a photo book. For me, the process of sorting and organising my photos into folders, and making a photo book, extends the enjoyment of the cruise. Narrowing the photos down to a handful of the best, can form the foundation for your coffee table photo book. These books can be a treasured keepsake of memories, a lovely reminder of your cruise, and a great way to show your trip to friends and family.

Webcam SeaScanner Positions of Cruise Ships

I have SeaScanner on my phone and I can call up almost any ship, anywhere in the world. Most ships will have a webcam on board to satisfy your cravings and stave off PCB as you track your favourite. I use it when I have booked my next cruise to follow the ship's progress until I board. There is nothing more exciting than waking up on cruise morning, checking the webcam and you can see your ship waiting for you, it's pure magic.

I can also use SeaScanner to reduce the impact of PCB, as I have a lot of friends on ships. I often screenshot the webcam pic and send it to them, somehow it feels like I am sharing in that moment at sea with them.

Always Have Your Next Cruise Booked

As a chronic suffer of PCB there is only one cure to this insidious condition. Don't panic leaving your cruise, you can perpetuate the vicious cruise cycle by starting to look around for your next cruise.

You can reduce the length or severity of PCB a few ways. Firstly, you can go to the future cruise desk while on board and put a deposit on your next cruise, or purchase future cruise credits. By doing this you can take advantage of any discounts or bonus such as On-Board Credit or reduced deposits. Be mindful that your decisions on holidays are not the same as the ones you would make while at home, so take a deep breath and maybe just buy future cruise credits instead of deciding on the itinerary.

Secondly, when you get home you can contact your travel agent to start the search for your next high seas adventure. If finances are a problem, you could start by saving small amounts of money each week, so when you have enough you can book your cruise and sail soon afterwards. Or you could also book your cruise a long time in advance, and pay it off incrementally before you leave.

Try Your Favourite Cocktails

I am cocktail Queen, I carry a folder on my phone with cocktail recipes both for on shore and at sea. I have made some lifetime friends of bartenders on cruise ships, so it helps me fight PCB if I chat to them online. You can relive your cruise experience by watching YouTube videos of master mixologists. A fun antidote to PCB is a Facebook page called the Tipsy Bartender, it can whet your creative cocktail appetite.

Explore YouTube
New ships post regular progress videos and launch updates online. You can find live reports or blogs from tech savvy passengers or crew members, on Facebook and YouTube, for example. Taking a virtual tour of your next cruise ship may just be the antidote to your PCB. Or check out my YouTube channel, Jules Cruise Companion, for some exciting videos of my latest travels on land and sea.

Make Towel Animals
The magic of a towel animal never grows old. I am a towel animal hoarder and end up with an entire Towel Zoo in my stateroom. I have kept so many to the point the stateroom attendant asked me if he could start breaking them down, he was running out of towels. I have even attended towel animal-folding classes.

Keep Yourself Busy
Make arrangements to go out and socialise, don't get into the work cycle routine. Catching up with people and sharing tales of your adventures allows you to relive the glory of the cruise.

Clean Your House Before You Leave
This does sound like a huge chore, but it is essential to come back to a nice house after your cruise. You can even make it part of the pre-cruise preparation and excitement. Unless you have a cleaner, returning to a messy house will exacerbate the PCB.

Do Some of Your Laundry on Your Cruise
By doing some laundry while cruising, you will postpone the huge laundry chore when you return home. When you have bags of dirty laundry, it is best to get started promptly, and it will reduce the smell and the sad visual reminder of your cruise's end.

Decorate Your Home Like a Cruise Ship
I know that this is a far-fetched idea and you would be using your cruise money to do this, but you could consider decorating your home with your favourite elements of a cruise ship. The closest I have come is choosing to live in a resort, ironically called *The Caribbean*.

Live Somewhere Touristy
It is a big decision, but one I have chosen. As I have just said, I choose to live in a resort. I live in a wonderful area, Queensland, Australia. I find it reduces my urge to escape because of the fantastic beaches, restaurants and attractions nearby. I don't have sea views from my home, but I do get to see cruise ships occasionally, as my area is now on some itineraries.

As we near the end of this book, I would like to talk more about my job as a professional cruise companion, in a little more depth.

You may want to go on a cruise but have no one to go with. You may have some health issues that you can deal with successfully at home, but are concerned about how to cope with on a cruise. Where can you turn for help?

My bespoke, personal and professional cruise companion service offers you the safety and security to have a wonderful, memorable and exciting cruise holiday.

What is a Cruise Companion?
A professional cruise companion is someone with nursing experience or who is a mature experienced traveller, able to assist you with mobility, guidance and support for hygiene and nutritional needs. A professional cruise companion can make your trip more comfortable and less daunting, allowing you to have a safer and more enjoyable travel experience.

Who Needs a Cruise Companion?
The type of person, couple, family with a special needs child, or group who may benefit from the services of a professional cruise companion, is almost endless.

- ☑ They could be someone who is anxious to travel alone or with family,
- ☑ Someone who has travelled in the past and has now lost the confidence,
- ☑ A couple who have travelled in the past and now one needs more help, guidance and support than the partner can provide,
- ☑ It could a be widow or widower who has health concerns and doesn't want to travel by themselves,
- ☑ It may be a family with a special needs child, who normally care for them independently at home, though find it hard to travel without additional support,
- ☑ Someone who is lonely or bored being by themselves or travelling by themselves,
- ☑ Someone with regrets, who has wanted to travel and didn't know how or didn't have anyone to go with,
- ☑ Someone with adult children who can't find the time in their hectic lives to travel with you,
- ☑ Someone whose decreased mobility might inhibit travelling alone or with family members,
- ☑ Someone who needs support and guidance to continue their cruise and travel dreams,
- ☑ Someone who wants to explore the world, connect with new people, have new experiences, though has health concerns where they don't think they will be able to travel by them self,
- ☑ Someone who wants to maintain a healthy active life exploring the world, ticking things off their bucket list, though it seems overwhelming to do with no support.

A professional cruise companion can assist you in various ways to realise you cruise dream. When you are in a wheelchair or use a wheelie walker, they will travel with you to handle luggage, assist with vehicle transfers, security checks, etc. You may need minimal guidance, supervision, prompting or support to keep you independent. This could be with medication, hygiene or a variety of daily needs and routines for safety reasons. This is where the professional cruise companion becomes an important part both in the preparation and the travel phase, with clear assessment of your specific needs and discussion about intervention strategies before you travel.

The advantage of travelling with a professional cruise companion is that they are trained to recognise medical emergencies and to act quickly and appropriately in these situations. They have the ability to foresee concerns ahead of time and to take measures to address these concerns, and have good problem-solving skills. Some safety strategies that we could put in place for you include what to do in the sun and heat or what to do when you get tired or fatigued. Travelling with a cruise companion is like travelling with a backup or emergency plan that will make it safer when you travel. Your cruise companion is great company to explore and share the amazing cruise experience.

How to Find a Cruise Companion
You could ask family and friends if they would accompany you on a cruise. Though they may not be professionally trained, they will be able to offer a level of support and reassurance.

Alternatively, you could hire a professional cruise companion. When you hire a cruise companion they will discuss your cruise expectations so that you are both on the same page. It is important to be honest with your expectations so that no one is disappointed. More information about my services can be found at my website: www.julescruisecompanion.com.au; or via email: julie@julescruisecompanion.com.au

Choosing a professional cruise companion begins with your initial contact, which may be via email, phone or in person.

This is the time to listen to your gut feelings. How you relate to the potential cruise companion? What is their demeanour? Do they seem flexible? How do you think the cruise companion will adapt to unexpected situations? What are your needs, your schedule, and your desires? Finding a professional cruise companion who meets all these needs should be your number one goal.

If it is not possible to have a personal meeting with the cruise companion, we will have a few lengthy conversations via Skype or Messenger. By having these conversations you will get an indication of how reasonable you will gel and how good a working relationship you will have with the cruise companion. When establishing any relationship it is important to have a sense of humour and not take yourself too seriously.

It is also important to be open and honest so that you can build a beneficial mutual understanding from the beginning. Another consideration that some people may have may relate to the age difference between you and the cruise companion. This may definitely be a factor that influences how you get along together, though with open minds and an adventurous spirit, an age difference is not going to be a barrier.

Take the leap of faith into the unknown, remember you only live once, so it is time to start travelling, pack your bags and have some life-altering experiences. Remember, you do not have an infinite lifespan. What is your strongest travel dream? What do you want to look back on your life and say, I wish I had done that? I suspect that dream would be to travel, and I would push it to even say to cruise. I wish you well on your cruise adventure, I hope to meet you one day on the high seas.

Keep an Open Heart and Open Mind.

Bon Voyage.

All Hands on Deck:
- Book another cruise while on-board and maybe get some bonuses
- Book when you get back home
- Turn your suitcase around ready for the next cruise.

Biography

I was born in Longreach, Central Western Queensland and grew up in Barcaldine, with two older brothers. My parents were hardworking people, though we were never well off. School holidays usually focused around visiting relatives and going on a lot of road trips, just to get anywhere.

My mother founded my love of travel as she encouraged me to travel on bus tours of Australia run by Youth Australia. These tours took a group of 14 to 17 year old country kids around Australia for a few weeks in the school holidays. I had a great time making new friends on each trip visiting Northern New South Wales, Canberra, and the Snow Fields. My mother would also take the family by bus to Brisbane every few years for the EKKA.

It was not uncommon for me to travel to Brisbane with school for work experience, Girl Guide Camps, or even alone to attend Drama Camps. My whole life involved travelling just to do normal everyday activities. To me, travel seemed a natural thing to do.

At age 21, I went on Fairstar The Funship to the Pacific Islands. At 22, I went on a Pub Crawl Bus Tour of Tasmania, and at 23, I had travelled Europe and was living in London. I came back to Australia for a few years before returning to England and living around Yorkshire until I was 32.

I became a single parent just before my son's 2nd birthday. After the usual life struggles, I started travelling with him when he was 7. We began with a road trip on the Dinosaur Trail in Central West Queensland, followed by a visit to the Snowfields in Northern New South Wales. His first plane ride was to Singapore at age 9, and his first cruise was at age 10 – from the U.S. to the Bahamas on Disney Wonder. During his teenage years we went on regular cruises, both locally and internationally. He left home at age 18, with the wanderlust spirit well and truly alive within him.

Over the years, I gained several qualifications, including Maternal and Child Welfare, Child Health Assistant, Enrolled Nurse, and finally becoming a Registered Nurse with a Bachelor Degree in Psychology (Honours). Aside from a short stint in the Private Sector, I have predominantly worked in Public Hospitals in Australia and England. I am privileged now to be working in Post Anaesthetic Care Unit (PACU) in a Tertiary Public Hospital, as I continue to build my own business sharing my knowledge and passion for travel and cruising.

After a 20 year gap between my first and second cruises, I made up for lost time as I have now been on over 30 cruises all around the world. My life philosophy of *Open Heart, Open Mind* is to go through life open to every joy and adventure. I have visited 48 countries so far, with many more to see. My aim is to cruise to as many countries as possible, inspiring others to follow their dreams and to create lifelong cruise memories.

Contact me: julie@julescruisecompanion.com.au

Visit my website: www.julescruisecompanion.com.au

Resources

Chronology of Ocean Liners and Cruise Ships:
worldtimeline.info/cruiseship

Cruise Lines International Association (CLIA) Research Centre:
www.cruising.org/about-the-industry/research

Cruising the Past – The Love Boat:
www.cruiselinehistory.com/about

Travelling with the Jones (Blog) – The History of Cruising:
www.travellingwiththejones.com/2014/06/26/the-history-of-cruising-and-cruise-ships

YouTube:

16 different looks in a 7kg carry on:
bit.ly/JCC7kgCarryOn

20kg checked luggage in a hybrid:
bit.ly/JCCCheckedHybrid

70 litre hybrid with 10 litre day pack:
bit.ly/JCCHybridLuggage

Blog Posts:

bit.ly/JCCCrazyThingsPeopleDoWhenCruising

bit.ly/JCCWhat2DoWhenYouDontLikeTenders

bit.ly/JCCWhyTravelIsGood4You

Bucket List

Name_____ **Date**_____

Priority

3 Countries I want to visit

1._____ High Medium Low
2._____ High Medium Low
3._____ High Medium Low

2 Activities I want to do

1._____
_____
_____
_____

2._____
_____
_____
_____
_____

2 Ways I will achieve activity 1

1._____
_____
_____
2._____
_____
_____
_____

2 Ways I will achieve activity 2

1._____
_____
_____
2._____
_____
_____
_____

12 . Resources

Cruise Packing List

Name_____ Cruise Date_____
Cruise Line_____ Cruise Ship_____

WOMEN
- [ ] 1 or 2 Formal Cocktail Outfits
- [ ] 3 Casual Dining Outfits
- [ ] 4 Dresses including a Maxi Dress
- [ ] Slacks
- [ ] 6-8 Underwear/Bras Undershirt/Socks/Hosiery
- [ ] 2/3 Scarves/Wrap/Pashmina
- [ ] 1-2 Swim over shirt Sarong

MEN
- [ ] Shirts Polo/Oxford
- [ ] A Sports Jacket or Business Suit
- [ ] 3 Casual Ding Dress Shirts
- [ ] Short – Khaki or Bermuda
- [ ] Long Pants
- [ ] 6-8 Underwear/socks
- [ ] 2/3 Ties

BOTH
- [ ] 2 Sets multipurpose sportswear/pyjamas
- [ ] 1 Sweatshirt
- [ ] 2 Sweat pants
- [ ] 1 Raincoat/Spray jacket/Overcoat
- [ ] 2 Light Neutral Coloured Sweaters
- [ ] 2 Jeans
- [ ] 3 Casual Shorts
- [ ] 4 T-Shirt/Casual Shirt (not strong prints)
- [ ] Dress Shoes
- [ ] 1 Casual Shoes/Loafers (walking shoes)
- [ ] 1 Pair Sandal
- [ ] 1 Pair Flip Flop/Jandal
- [ ] 1 Pair of Sneakers

HYGIENE PACK
- [ ] Toothbrush
- [ ] Toothpaste
- [ ] Mouthwash
- [ ] Dental Floss
- [ ] Comb & Brush
- [ ] Shampoo & Conditioner
- [ ] Soap (Small)
- [ ] Makeup/Cosmetics (minimal)
- [ ] Eye Care Cream
- [ ] Hair Styling Products
- [ ] Nail Clippers
- [ ] Q-Tips
- [ ] Tissues
- [ ] Deodorant
- [ ] Razor & Shaving Lotion
- [ ] Perfume/Cologne
- [ ] Tweezers
- [ ] Feminine Hygiene Products

MISCELLANEOUS
- [ ] Smartphone & Charger
- [ ] 2 pairs of sunglasses
- [ ] Watch
- [ ] Hat
- [ ] Pen
- [ ] TSA Locks & tags
- [ ] Luggage Scales
- [ ] International Power Converter
- [ ] Power Board
- [ ] USB charger and Cable
- [ ] Camera
- [ ] Memory Cards
- [ ] Headphones
- [ ] Laptop & Cord
- [ ] Batteries
- [ ] Highlighter Pen
- [ ] 1 umbrella or light plastic poncho
- [ ] 1 pair of reef Shoes
- [ ] Light Back Pack
- [ ] Beach/Pool Tote
- [ ] Water Bottle (collapsible)
- [ ] Laundry detergent
- [ ] Peg-less clotheslines & S-Hooks or Suction Hooks
- [ ] Safety Pins

MEDIAL PACK
- [ ] Personal Prescription Medication
- [ ] First Aid Kit
- [ ] Simple Pain Relief
- [ ] Cold/Sinus Medication
- [ ] Antiemetic
- [ ] Motion Sickness Medication
  - Sea-band
  - Dramamine
  - Essential oils
  - Ginger
- [ ] Broad Spectrum Antibiotic
- [ ] Diarrhoea Medication
- [ ] Vitamins
- [ ] Insect repellent
- [ ] Over the counter medications
  - Antacids
  - Tylenol
  - Neosporin
  - Antibiotic Ointment
  - Anti-Fungal Ointment
- [ ] Band Aids
- [ ] Sunscreen

OPTIONAL
- [ ] Plastic Bag
- [ ] Ear Plugs
- [ ] Eye Mask
- [ ] Hand Sanitizer (small)
- [ ] Room Sanitizer or freshener (non-Aerosol)
- [ ] Lysol Disinfectant wipes
- [ ] Selfie Stick
- [ ] Travel Alarm Clock
- [ ] Playing cards
- [ ] 1 Swim Goggles
- [ ] 1 set of swim flippers
- [ ] Over the door storage hanger
- [ ] Binoculars
- [ ] Post-it Notes
- [ ] Books/Puzzle Book
- [ ] Kindle & Charger
- [ ] Flashlight (if you don't have a Smartphone)

EXTRAS
- [ ] _____
- [ ] _____
- [ ] _____
- [ ] _____
- [ ] _____
- [ ] _____

A last minute reminder of what NOT to pack, DO NOT take illegal drugs, weapons like firearms or knives, anything that could cause a fire, no electric jugs, hairdryers, candles, etc.

BON VOYAGE